C000088193

NEIL WILSON PUBLISHING • Glasgow • Scotland

To my mother Mary Hannah Elizabeth Murray,
my lifelong purveyor of tender encouragement who entered this world in 1921 as a
Crimins.

Also, to all long lost Irish members of that
family, whoever, wherever they may be.

Published by Neil Wilson Publishing Ltd
309 The Pentagon Centre
36 Washington Street
GLASGOW G3 8AZ
Tel: 041-221-1117
Fax: 041-221-5363

The moral right of the author has been asserted.
A catalogue record for this book is available from the
British Library.
ISBN 1-897784-33-3

Typeset in 8.5/9pt Formata by Face to Face Design
Services, Glasgow

Printed in Scotland by Scotprint Ltd, Musselburgh

ACKNOWLEDGEMENTS

It goes without saying that a book like this cannot be written without the aid of a great many people. On top of the great fun I have had visiting Ireland in the past, the extra kindness I received while researching this book will always be cherished.

In particular I would like to thank: Ms Ide Ni Thuama of the Royal Irish Academy; Dr Richard Sharp, Oxford University; John Burgass, Librarian, Merton College, Oxford; Miss P Kernaghan, Deputy Keeper of the Records, Public Record Office of Northern Ireland and Ms EDL Lumsden for their kind permission in allowing me to quote from the Samual Lumsden papers D649/11-14; Jack Gamble of Emerald Isle Books, Belfast; John Ryan, Barry Walsh, Michael Borre and Cathal O'Farrell of Irish Distillers, Dublin; Barry Crockett at Midleton Distillery; Douglas Deane, the North Mall bottling plant, Cork; Frank McHardy, Denis Higgins, John McLernon and the gatekeeper at Bushmills Distillery; Caroline Davey (formerly) and Heidi Cohu, now of Campbell Distillers; John Harte and Noel Sweeney of Cooley Distillers; Robert Mitchell and Peter Dunne of Mitchell & Son, Dublin; Kevin Abrook of Cantrell & Cochrane, Dublin and Joe Scally of Irish Mist at Tullamore; Gordon Wright and Neil Clapperton, of Wm Cadenhead, Campbeltown and Edinburgh; Dr Nicholas Morgan of the United Distillers Archive, Edinburgh; Jonathan Driver of United Distillers, London; Jamie Graham and the Board of Directors of Berry Bros & Rudd, London; Peter O'Connor of Baileys, Dublin; Tom Keaveney of Gilbey's, Ireland; Paul Hyland of Mooney's and P.J Brennan of Brennan's, Monasterevan; Eddie Nevin of The Vineyard, Galway; Philip and Mark Russell of The Elk, Dundonald; my man John, the illicit distiller somewhere in Co. Donegal; Morton McKnight and Maynard Hanna of Distillery FC; Bea Tom of The Buena Vista Cafe, San Francisco; Oliver Dillon of the Bunratty Mead Co and Michael Sohel of Pondicherry International, Leeds; Mr Brian Lawson, former sexton of St Michan's Church, Dublin; Margaret Bridgman of Halewood Vintners, West Yorks; John Layden and the sixth form Latin students of

Wellingborough School; Billy Walker of Burn Stewart Distillers, Airdrie; Michael Sullivan and Karen Alexander of James McCabe Ltd of Craigavon; Dr Jim Swan of R.R. Tatlock and Thomson, Glasgow, and Jimmy Lang, Becky Calcraft, Howard Buchanan, Sue Westall and Diana Crook. My very warmest thanks go to Christina Holmes, whose late husband John did so much to record the history of Monasterevan Distillery, for being such a charming and good-natured guide around the remains of the old distillery at a time of great personal sadness.

Most of all I would like to give a big hug and kiss to my young son James for being such a funny and understanding companion on our sojourn around Ireland's past and present distilleries, and for all the time he has merrily got on with things at home, allowing me to somehow complete this book in time for publication. I'm also indebted to my other wonderful children, Tabitha and David, for likewise so uncomplainingly taking second place to this labour of love when there was vitally important shopping and cricket practice to be done!

CONTENTS

INTRODUCTION

For a people so friendly and who, in any of the thousands of bars that can be found in every village and town throughout the land, will engage you in lively debate on any topic under the sun and expound their views with a courteous freedom, the Irish are also very fond of keeping their secrets.

Until the publication of this book, perhaps their biggest secret of all was Irish whiskey. While the rest of the world has been allowed to sample only Jamesons and Bushmills as works of the Irish distiller's art, the Irish have been able to rejoice daily in the latter-day *uisce beatha*, the water of life, which although not aiming to challenge the best established whisk(e)ys in the world, is unquestionably their peer.

Who in Britain, the USA, South Africa, Germany, Australia, New Zealand or any other whiskey drinking nation has ever been fortunate enough to discover the truly astonishing delights of a Powers or a Redbreast: two whiskeys with such succulent pot still character that you nose and drink a part of Ireland's very soul every time you put them to your lips? Regrettably, few people have had the chance.

This, quite remarkably, is the first book ever to take a drinker on a detailed tour around all Ireland's whiskeys, no matter how common or obscure. Other books have been written on Irish whiskey but they have covered only its turbulent history, never its produce.

I have ensured that my *Irish Whiskey Almanac* has gone beyond that historical perspective. My single aim in this book is to act as a personal guide to anyone who wishes to know something, not only about its history, but also (and perhaps more importantly to those who will be spending good money on a bottle!), the character of the whiskey and why it tastes the way it does. After all, no whiskey in the world is made in such a complicated manner as the Irish variety and for the very first time some of the major secrets of why Irish whiskey has such a distinctive flavour will be revealed.

The reader may not agree with all my tasting notes. They are, after all, a subjective view. But I am sure he or she will understand my standpoint and use these notes to either try out or stay away from certain brands. Whiskey is not an inexpensive commodity and therefore my impartiality should help you in selecting only what suits you best.

Over recent years I have written more in newspapers and magazines than any other writer on Irish whiskey, and not always through shamrock-tinted spectacles. Irish Distillers know I will never be content until they allow more of their brands to become available throughout the world. I hope this book awakens people's interest so that it is not only me pleading to give pot still a chance. I feel sure the day is not too far away.

But I cannot be too harsh; Irish Distillers is a commercial enterprise and must put its money where it feels it will most bear fruit. And they *do* produce some truly wonderful whiskeys which I have endeavoured not to make too wonderful for words!

I am lucky. My work as a whisk(e)y writer takes me to distilleries all over the world and there is something about Ireland which is special. It may be my Irish blood from a couple of generations back; it may be the softly contoured land of pastel greens; it may be the warmth of the people; it may be the enchantment felt by the discovery of yet another facet of a whiskey you thought you already intimately knew. It is probably all those things.

Through the pages of this book I want to take you on a special journey and share my very good fortune with you.

Jim Murray
Wellingborough
England
July 1994

THE ORIGINS OF IRISH WHISKEY

Inevitably, no matter in how detailed or brief a manner you tell the story of Irish whiskey the reader will be searching for an answer to the obvious question: when did it all begin?

Unless an ancient document, previously undiscovered, comes to light regarding the origins of distilling in Ireland, a single fact will always remain: nobody really knows. Over the years there have been many claimed instances of Irish whiskey being mentioned in ancient texts. But, to date, all my researches have drawn a blank. Stories which have been accepted as gospel and recounted in many books, booklets and pamphlets all founder on the hard rocks of fact and few of them stand up to close scrutiny.

A problem with the telling of tales down through the centuries is that they tend to be romanticised, or bent and moulded into a shape which will be most appreciated by the targeted listener or reader. Frequently these stories serve merely as commercial propoganda. It has ever been thus with Irish whiskey.

It has been claimed, for instance, even by the great whiskey guru of the late 19th and early 20th century, J.A. Nettleton, that it was first mentioned by soldiers of Henry II when they invaded Ireland in 1174. But Nettleton only appeared to be apeing the great Samuel Morewood, whose gloriously titled *A Philosphical and Statistical History of the Inventions and Customs of Ancient and Modern Nations in the Manufacture of Inebriating Liquors* of 1838, is still, in my opinion, the best work of its kind ever written. Although Morewood painted a vivid picture of drinking the world over, he was a Dubliner who was understandably given to venting national pride.

So far, I have been unable to discover the source of Henry II's alleged connection with whiskey. The most likely candidate to have had early connections would have been Giraldus De Barri, now known as Gerald of Wales; then simply as Cambrensis, a monk of breathtaking self-importance who was close to the king and whose own relations took part in the invasion. Cambrensis' dislike of the Irish bordered on the manic and in his first book on them and the country, *The History and Topography of Ireland (Topographia Hibernica)*, he was at pains to describe them as 'treacherous, cruel, dishonest' — and those were the kinder insults. If he could find any fault with them he would. Oddly, though, at no stage did he mention any habit of drinking *uisce beatha*, the Celtic words meaning 'water of life' which eventually came to be known as whiskey. He talks about an abundance of wine being available, all of it imported, and much milk and honey, but he does not mention ale or even distilled ale, which would have been the forerunner to whiskey.

Soon after his *Topographia Hibernica* was published, by popular demand Cambrensis wrote an account in 1188 of Henry II's conquest of Ireland, the *Expugnatio Hibernica*. And again, though going into great detail and taking delight in repeating many of the insults he had already heaped on the Irish people, the habit of making or drinking whiskey was not amongst them. In fairness to this revered monk (revered outside Ireland, that is), he did make observations on their way of life beyond the bestial and it does seem strange that had whiskey making been in evidence, he chose not to mention it.

My research eventually led me to the unlikely setting of Merton College, the oldest seat of learning in Oxford. There they have an original copy of the 14th-century *Rosa Anglica*, (by John of Gaddesden, the foremost physician of his day who was mentioned in the prologue of Chaucer's *Canterbury Tales)* and for the next three centuries the standard work which all physicians consulted. Apparently, there is in existence a 15th-century Irish translation of this work in which the word 'whiskey' appears and is described as being used as a tool to aid the healing of paralysis of the tongue: 'Rub the tongue and wash frequently with whiskey...Let the whiskey be rubbed often on the back of the head, the tongue and the paralysed limb...'

However, on searching through the original edition at Merton, where Gaddesden himself studied, I could find no reference at all to whiskey. Instead, in the handwritten Latin, it appears as 'aqua vitae', which also means 'water of life'. Furthermore, Gaddesden actually revealed how to prepare aqua vitae. It was made from wine, not grain, and although herbs were added to form a compounded liquor, cereal grains such as barley and oats, were not.

Likewise, beware that some books suggest that when Sir Thomas Savage, who overlorded the lands which now include Bushmills distillery, fortified his troops prior to battle with the English by topping them up with 'Uisce Beatha'. It was in fact aqua vitae, according to the noted Elizabethan Thomas Campion. In any case, noblemen like Savage would have drunk wine as a matter of habit, regarding aqua vitae as too coarse and beneath their station.

Tall tales with foundations as soft and murky as an Irish peat bog are all that exist of the earliest popular stories regarding Irish whiskey. For years I was of the opinion that the art of distillation had been brought to Scotland from Ireland by the early Christian holy men of those dark ages between the retreat of the Romans and the invasion of England by the Normans. As my investigations continued, those beliefs began to vanish. I was surprised to discover that not only was there no mention whatsoever of distillation in the ancient Irish Brehon laws, but there was not even a word for such common distilling artefacts as 'still' or 'still worm' in the Irish language.

But this is, after all, a subject of some confusion and contradiction. I have stated already that Cambrensis made no mention of distilling or brewing. How does that tally, then, with the fact that the brewing of ale in Ireland is clearly recorded by Jonus in his *Life of St Columbanus* written between 589 and 640AD? 'When the hour of refreshment approached, the minister endeavoured to serve about the ale which is bruised from the juice of wheat and barley...' So if Cambrensis is mistaken here, or simply did not bother to record the practice, could the same be said for distilling?

While Cambrensis had some strange and unpleasant stories to tell about the people of Erin, he does not pick up on a story told in the *Annals of Ulster* of 1013 which mentions people drinking themselves to death, although the deadly liquor is not named. Two annals written long after the time of Cambrensis, the

Annals of the Four Masters and the *Annals of Clonmacnoise* independently tell the same story about Richard Magranell. In the latter: 'AD 1405, Richard Magranell, chieftain of Moyntyreolas, died at Christmas by taking a surfeit of aqua vitae...it was not aqua vitae to him but aqua mortis'. This is the first time aqua vitae, in any form, is mentioned in any of Ireland's ancient documents.

But, again, there is no evidence of the distilling of grain spirit, unlike Scotland where, in the year 1494, the first ever mention of whiskey is made. In the Scottish Exchequer Rolls is found the following entry: 'To Friar John Cor, by order of the King, to make aquavitae, viii bolls of malt...' Here both aqua vitae and malt are mentioned together, an irrefutable case, at last.

For real proof, the Irish have to wait even longer than that. An Act of Parliament apparently passed in Drogheda in 1556 and referred to in 1620 states '...in Ireland, for the prices of wines extends not to aqua vitae, but there is a statute made in the fourth yeare of Phillip and Mary, here in Ireland....that recites the consumption of graine in making of aqua vitae, and that it is not profitable daily drunk....under paine of Imprisonment at the Deputie's pleasure...' What worries me about this reference is that the fourth year of Phillip and Mary did not fall until 1558. Even so, what is clear is that by the early Tudor period there was concern already about the effects which grain aqua vitae — whiskey — was having on the Irish population.

This was further underlined through by-laws introduced in Galway in 1585: 'That a more straighter order be taken to barr the making of aqua vite of corn than hereunto hath beene used, for that the same is a consumation of all the provition of corne in the Commonwealth. That the aqua vite that is sould in town ought rather to be called aqua mortis to poyson the people than comfort them in any good sorte.' Maybe the whiskey made in Galway was poison. But could these measures not have been made in the self-interest of wealthy merchants? Galway was a major port which did such an amount of business with Spain that a Spanish quarter grew up within the town. And one of the principal imports from Spain was wine.

It seems certain, therefore, that the making and drinking of whiskey was widespread throughout Ireland by the 16th century. The art of distillation was known in Ireland by the 14th century, and possibly before by monks for the purpose of healing. The making of ale was a common practice by circa 600AD, so despite the fact that neither Bede nor Cambrensis felt fit to mention this remarkable alchemy, it might still be assumed that somewhere between the year 600AD and the 1300s the two crafts of brewing and distilling were carried out together. Incidentally, the undated *Red Book of Ossory* which is thought to be 14th-century, mentions the art of distilling of wine as well.

If the monks did make aqua vitae from grain, they kept very quiet about it. And so did the merchants, because according to Morewood, in 1300 wheat, oats, malt and ale were exported to Scotland to replenish Edward I's invading army. Aqua vitae, whether derived from grain or wine, was not listed.

It remains an enigma, one over which I shall continue to puzzle and to which one day I hope to find an answer.

A Brief Outline of Irish Distilling

The period between the late 16th century and the early 19th century was one of extreme confusion as regards the making of Irish whiskey. English-based governments saw the increase in popularity and availability of this spirit as one of the main reasons for the continuing civil unrest. At the same time it was realised by those governments that there were benefits to be had from this widespread craft.

It is perhaps surprising that as the making of whiskey flourished in Ireland during the reign of Elizabeth I (1558-1603) — who was apparently quite fond of it — the Queen, whose household was in a permanent state of financial difficulty, did not recognise a new opportunity to raise revenue from taxing distilling.

Instead, it was not until Christmas Day 1661 that the Government gave the people a present they hardly wanted — a tax of four pence on every gallon of whiskey distilled. Poteen making began on the Boxing Day!

With immediate effect, a new Government department was set up in Dublin: the Excise. For the first 100 years the department had very limited success.

Distillers would declare only what they could get away with, while many declared nothing at all and took to the hills to make their spirit. Corruption was rife, with MPs and powerful landowners able to produce what they wanted tax-free, or undertake to collect the duty from others and divert it into their own pockets. In 1761 the Excise Department, or Revenue Board as it was known, was revamped. It had more powers than of old and more teeth to bare. Until 1823 the scene in Ireland was in a constant state of flux with the rates of taxation being changed, it seemed, every other month. With distillers bogged down in regulations, those who became either too entangled in them, or avoided them altogether, faced fines and imprisonment if the Excisemen, the 'gaugers', found them out.

In that year an Act of Parliament was passed to make distilling a much simpler and more equitable affair for those with bigger stills, and an outright illegal one for those with stills which held less than 40 gallons. Anything smaller was considered small enough to conceal.

The making of illicit and legal whiskey had never been so far apart. By the end of the 18th century there were some 2000 stills in operation in Ireland where whiskey had become the national spirit in a very big way.

Morewood, on opening his section on drinking in his homeland underlined this point commenting: 'In Ireland ... distilling is carried out to a greater extent than any other portion of the world of equal magnitude and ... forms a branch of great commercial importance and enterprise ...'

Indeed it did. Some who decided to distil legally tried to raise the capital to set themselves up as large concerns. The most successful were the four big Dublin distillers: John Power, John Jameson, George Roe and William Jameson. Theirs was considered the finest whiskey in all Ireland. Along with other Irish distillers' exports, their products were sold throughout the British Empire and beyond and their success was boosted quite unexpectedly when the *phylloxera vastatrix* louse decimated the vines in the Cognac region of France in 1872, making French wines and particularly brandy, almost impossible to obtain.

Irish whiskey then outsold its Scottish counterpart

on account of the unmalted barley used exclusively in Irish whiskey which made it a lighter spirit. Both Irish and Scotch became popular drinks with the mon-eyed classes as stocks of brandy dried up and the pre-prandial became a Scotch or Irish and soda. But as Irish whiskey appeared to be on the verge of tak-ing the world market by storm, four totally uncon-nected events took a stranglehold on its progress.

The first occurrence was in the unlikely form of a Capuchin Friar, Father Mathew, who, during the 1840s and 50s swept through the country turning people against his perceived evils of the demon drink. Tem-perance societies were set up in their hundreds throughout Ireland and sinners, seeing the error of their ways (and no doubt with much encouragement from their long-suffering wives), were persuaded to turn their backs on whiskey, beer and stout for ever. Such was the fever pitch at his rallies that in two visits to Dublin he claimed to have signed up 75,000 con-verts to his Total Abstinence Movement. When he began the crusade in 1838 there were some 21,000 drinking outlets in Ireland and more money was be-ing spent on drink than was good for the Irish economy and its people's health. However, within six years of his work commencing, that number was down by more than a third to just over 13,000. The small, provincial distiller began to look financial ruin in the face.

The second came with the development of blended whiskey. Ironically it was a French-born Irishman and exciseman Aeneas Coffey and to a lesser extent a Scot, Robert Stein, who worked in a Dublin distillery, who accidentally set the ball rolling. Coffey had tried to sell to the Irish distillers his design for a more effi-cient continuous still which made cheaper grain spirit, but contained far less flavour. They rejected his pro-posals out of hand since they wished to keep Irish whiskey light, but full flavoured, and produced by the traditional pot still method.

Meanwhile in Scotland, a spirit merchant and agent for The Glenlivet Distillery called Andrew Usher, had no such reservations. He experimented with a mix-ture of Scottish malt whisky and grain whisky from a Coffey still to produce a number of blends, one of which, Green Stripe, is still produced today. His commitment to the new process, in around 1853, was the green flag for other blenders like Dewar and Buchanan to begin to sell their whiskies around the world. The age of the 'whisky baron' had begun.

In Ireland there was no such progress. They looked upon blended whisky with outright disdain, but suddenly became caught up with its effects when their export sales began losing out to 'Scotch', as the Scottish blends were becoming known. Also, the very whiskey which they went to such pains to protect was now being sold by middlemen as blends of traditional pot still and grain whiskey.

The situation became so bad that in 1879 the four Dublin distillers joined forces to publish a book called *Truths About Whisky* (sic). Very often people ordering Irish whiskey had been shocked to discover that it was relatively tasteless. In fact the blenders, without the distillers' consent, had been using perhaps only 20% pot still whiskey in the make-up. The book called for the banning of this practice. Part of their defence was the fact that the Scottish Bo'ness Distillery Company sued Londonderry publican John Magee for refusing to pay for a cask of whiskey which he claimed was adulterated:

> The order of the cask from the Company's Belfast agent, and its delivery in the usual way, having been proved, the defendant said that he had opened the cask the day he had got it, and gave about a glass and a half of the spirit to a boy named Bradley. After drinking it Bradley leaped clean up off the ground, then threw himself down on his mouth and nose, and endeavoured to knock his brains out. When lying on the gound he wanted to eat the flesh of his arms ...

The inference by the authors was that a spirit made in Ireland, perhaps from potatoes, had been added to the whisky.

Although the magistrate found in favour of the publican, a Government commission designed to sort out the 'What is Whisky?' question decided that grain spirit could also be called whisky provided it was matured for long enough. From then on the Irish dis-

tillers had un uphill battle against the Scotch produc-
ers and only Cork Distilleries seemed keen on marketing a blend, although with little of the zeal that
had gone into the by then world-famous Scotch
brands.

Even so, Irish whiskey still had a healthy market in
many parts of the Empire and the United States. But
those, too, were soon to be lost. The US market was
placed beyond them by the enforcement of Prohibition in 1920 which continued until 1933. Only com-
paratively small amounts managed to breach the
blockade. Worse still, the Irish War of Independence
in 1916 resulted firstly in the partition of the country
and then in civil war between 1919 and 1921. When
a trade war began between the new Free State and
Britain, the Irish whiskey industry was going to be a
sure-fire casualty. The British and Empire markets including Canada, South Africa, Australia, New Zealand
and India were from that date beyond the Irish distillers' reach.

Many distilleries died out. For some like Monasterevan and Wexford, it was a quick end. For others,
like Kilbeggan, Comber and Tullamore, it was a slow
death stretching into the mid 1950s. By the time the
the trade embargoes had ended and Prohibition had
been repealed only a few distillers like John Jameson
and Power had sufficient stocks to allow them to try
to rekindle the market. But their commercial strength
had been greatly weakened and an entire generation
had gone without the pleasure of tasting Irish whiskey. There was plenty of Scotch, though, taking its
place.

In 1966, however, a momentous decision was
reached. The few remaining distilling companies in
the Republic, Jameson, Powers and Cork Distilleries,
decided to combine forces to create the Irish Distillers Company. Their aim was to pool resources and
fight for some share of the world market. It was not
the first time distilleries had joined forces in this way.
Cork Distilleries had begun as a merger of a number
of distilleries, and when Irish Distillers acquired Ulster's last distillery, Bushmills in the early 1970s, every
Irish whiskey brand was being marketed under one
corporate banner. But Irish whiskey as a whole was
stationary. The Irish Distillers Group at that time had a

very unimpressive track record in that most vital of sales areas — export. It was regarded in Ireland as a company performing well below expectations and was often criticised. As the company grew weaker, takeover became inevitable.

Between 1987 and 1989 Irish Distillers found themselves in the centre of the most dramatic tug-of-war in the Republic's industrial history. On the one hand was a company called GC&C Brands, jointly owned by two Irish companies, Gilbey's of Ireland and Cantrell & Cochrane. (Guinness had quietly teamed up with them to strengthen the bid.) These companies were already the subsidiaries of two enormous British concerns: Grand Metropolitan and Allied Lyons, but the successful buyer was eventually the French group Pernod-Ricard (after a number of bruising business encounters). On their victory Shane Jameson, the last member of any of the old family distillers in Dublin or Cork, resigned.

Had GC&C won, the brands would have been broken up into two camps: Gilbey's on the one hand and Cantrell & Cochrane backed by Guinness on the other. That would have meant massive marketing of a number of whiskey brands throughout the world. Instead, Pernod-Ricard decided upon a policy of putting all their marketing clout behind Jameson and Bushmills on the world stage, leaving the others almost exclusively for home consumption. The monopoly was set to continue.

However, that is not quite the case now with the emergence of the Cooley Distillery near Dundalk. Irish Distillers tried and failed to take over and close down the Co. Louth distillery and while doing so, they offloaded their Tullamore Dew brand to Cantrell & Cochrane. Again, Irish distillers have to fight it out in the market amongst themselves.

But the market has changed, as people's perceptions and expectations have moved a little higher. Irish whiskey, whether from Midleton, Cooley or Bushmills, is at last being seen again for what it was clearly recognised as over a century ago: a very high class product of great finesse. Now all these distillers must work to ensure that the future will be a lot kinder to Irish whiskey than its past.

THE MAKING OF IRISH WHISKEY

There is a popular misconception regarding Ireland and its most glorious product. And maybe the very fact that it is a whiskey making country has helped confuse matters. Many people outside the industry believe Irish whiskey is made in similar conditions to those in Scotland. That may be true to an extent up at Bushmills in Co Antrim, just a couple of miles from a pounding sea where drizzle always seems to hang in the air, and to a lesser degree at Cooley, where the distillery nestles in the foothills of the mountains of Mourne. But it is certainly not true at the greatest of all Ireland's distilleries, Midleton in Co Cork.

Just a few miles along the road to the east of the city, Midleton sits on the same latitude as Hitchin near London, rather than the Highlands of Scotland. At Midleton the sea laps nearby but there are no mountains, just gentle hills and the occasional palm tree thriving in the serenity of the Gulf Stream breeze. Snow falls but a few days in winter, rarely lying for long on the ground and the warehouses in which the whiskey is stored are often clammy and humid rather than dank and freezing.

You would expect, then, the fruits of Midleton's giant stills to be markedly different to anything produced elsewhere, and they are. But, oddly, although the temperate weather does have some effect on maturation and the outcome of the whiskey, it is the distilling practice carried out within the Midleton complex which has the biggest say in its character. In Scotland it could be argued that the wood in whisky maturation has the greatest influence overall: not so at Midleton.

I can think of no other distillery in the world which is as complex as the plant in Co Cork. When the new distillery was designed and built it had to produce a range of whiskeys which, when blended, would form similar characters to the original whiskeys produced at Jameson in Bow Street, Power of John's Lane, the original Midleton and, to some extent, Tullamore.

By the time the new Midleton distillery went into operation in March 1975 things had already been made a lot easier. For a start the type of whiskey was now lighter in style with much of the heavy oiliness removed. This process had been adopted in the late 1960s by all the distilleries as they battled to improve not only quality control but also their standing amongst whiskey drinkers throughout the world who preferred the perceptibly cleaner Scotch. Also, the content of the pot still was now simply the mash from malted and unmalted barley. That had not always been the case.

During the late 19th and early 20th centuries five types of grain were commonly used: malt as 30-50% by weight, barley as 30-40%, oats as 20-30%, wheat as 5-10% and rye as 3-6%. Because of this low amount of malted barley, the mashing process — where the ground grain is mixed with hot water — used to take a long time with lower temperatures initially used than was common in Scotland. This would have added greatly to the oiliness. Gradually, wheat and rye were dropped from the recipe although oats were still in use until the 1960s. But that changed as well with the incorporation of more unmalted barley. By the time the new Midleton plant swung into operation, oats, like rye and wheat were, from a pot still point of view, a thing of the past. This has meant that the taste of pure pot still Irish whiskey has also changed somewhat over the years; hardly any difference between now and the early 1970s, but by some margin from a century ago.

Midleton not only makes pure pot still but also, when required, a pure single malt and also grain whiskey from column stills. What is so remarkable is that Midleton makes several styles of each type, be it pot still, pure malt or single grain, and its range of whiskeys covers a wider spectrum than any other distillery I know in the world.

Contents apart, the first stages of the making of all types of whiskey at Midleton, Bushmills and Cooley are identical. First, the grain is crushed into a powder called 'grist'. This is then added to hot water, which at Bushmills is 63C/145F and at a slightly cooler Midleton is 60C/140F, in a metal vessel called the mash tun and then slowly stirred by mechanical means. The natural sugars present in the grist and other solubles dissolve into the water which is then drained off. This process is repeated twice before the spent solids, called 'draff', are removed. The water from the third mashing is held back and used with the first water from the next mashing using fresh grist. In other words, the first water of any mashing contains a percentage of water from the the previous mash, which goes some way to creating a form of consistency.

The liquid containing the dissolved sugars and grain, called 'wort', is then pumped into a set of vessels called washbacks, or at Midleton, 'fermenters'. At this point, yeast is added which reacts with the sugars to produce a beer-like liquid, orange-brown in colour at about 8.5% alcohol by volume (abv). When fermentation has run its course and the liquid quietens from a foaming, frothing cauldron to a tranquil, murky lake, it is then pumped through to the stills.

It is at this juncture that things begin to change. At Bushmills the wash is distilled three times in medium-sized pot stills, each time with increasing alcoholic strength as the distillate becomes lighter in density. At Cooley the malt is distilled twice, as is the practice amongst most Scottish distilleries, thus producing a slightly heavier spirit. At Midleton, however, the fate awaiting the wash depends on precisely the kind of whiskey they want to produce.

If the wash is to be pumped directly into the large pot stills, it is likely to be a mixture of malted and unmalted barley. Midleton hasn't produced any pure malt whiskey since 1988, although in the next few years there is every chance they will distil some more to replenish their stocks.

For pot still whiskey the grist will have been made up from anything within the parameters of 60% unmalted barley and 40% malt, or from a straight 50/50 split. From this range of mixes three types of whiskey can be produced: light pot still; medium/modified (known as Midleton Mod Pot); or heavy. Once, though no more, they made a fourth, even heavier version called Trad (Traditional) Pot. At any other distillery the results will be achieved in the final part of the distilling process. After all three distillations, the stillman can produce a heavy whiskey by capturing a greater portion of the latter part of the distillate 'run' which contains some of the heavier oils. If he requires a lighter spirit he will select a more central portion of the run will be selected. The result is not only a lighter spirit, but also one that is higher in alcoholic strength.

There are further processes at Midleton to complicate matters. As well as the use of the three pot stills (wash, intermediate and spirit) some of the whiskey is distilled through two column stills designed primarily for the making of grain whiskey, more of which I will explain later.

These stills, like most column stills around the world, are pretty boring to look at. But at Midleton they are quite fascinating because they are linked to the pot stills so that some of the impure spirits, called 'low wines', which runs off from the wash pot still, is fed through both column stills before being pumped back into the second (intermediate) pot still and then into the final, spirit pot still. In the intermediate still it rejoins the distillate considered to be of the highest quality from the first run from the wash still. Meanwhile in the first column still (the wash column) the impure spirit from the first pot still does not make its long, complicated journey alone: it is mixed with the impure spirit from the intermediate and spirit pot stills.

By the time the mid-cut of the run from the spirit still is filled into cask it will have been distilled at least three times, and a small percentage of it five times. It is the most complicated whiskey making system in the world. And it is repeated when Midleton Mod Pot is produced, except that the stillman does not select such a narrow band of the mid-cut from all three stills. Only when Midleton produce a heavy pot still whiskey are the column stills dispensed with altogether. With so many different types of pot still whiskey to choose from, the blender is then able to select different styles, at different ages, for different brands.

Midleton also produces the grain whiskey required not only for their own blends but also Bushmills'. Sometimes the grain is made from a mixture of malted (20-25%) and unmalted (80-75%) barley. This tends to produce a more fully flavoured grain whiskey than when they use wheat or maize. Originally the distillery used only maize, but it was found to be more economic to convert to wheat, which gives a softer, sometimes spicier taste on maturation. However, in the spring of 1994 Midleton switched back to maize. Although it is more expensive to import, it was then considered a more economic proposition when the distillery was working flat out. The great problem with wheat is that there is no husk when it is milled and after mashing it leaves a mess which is time-consuming to clear up. And even in an Irish distillery, time is money.

Column stills, or patent stills as they are also known, are much more efficient than pot stills. They distil continuously, unlike pot stills which must been cleaned out after every charge. They also produce a purer, more alcohol-rich product, but like pot stills they are used to distil grain spirit three times. Sadly, their efficiency means they also remove the very oils which go to make pot still whiskey so flavoursome. When required these stills also make the spirit needed for the company's gin and vodka brands.

One of the great features of the Midleton distillery are the acres upon acres given over to warehousing. In Scotland, warehouses, or bonds, tend to be smaller than at Midleton and the system of stacking, or 'racking' the casks is also different. Usually in Scotland distillers rack their whisky in long rows side by side. At Midleton the casks are stacked upright on pallets which are then placed on top of each other, a process which is much less labour intensive. Theory suggests that the casks will have less air circulating around them and so maturation should be slower. So far this has not been noticeable, and with the climate at Midleton being generally warmer than the Highlands, maturation does take place at a slightly faster rate anyway.

Irish whiskey is matured more extensively in old sherry casks than in Scotland and the company's recent investment in buying brand new casks from bodegas in southern Spain has been vast. Also, for the maturation of the pot still whiskey, Irish Distillers claim to use the cheaper, ex-bourbon casks for a shorter period than Scottish distillers.

When whiskey matures in ex-sherry casks, the alcohols in the spirit leach out the sherry which has soaked into the wood and, depending on how long it is left to mature, also start working on the chemicals in the wood. When whiskey is filled into old bourbon casks, the bourbon they formerly held has no effect on the whiskey whatsoever. But since these bourbon casks have originally been charred, the spirit is able to find its way into the exposed, fresh wood via the thousands of miniscule cracks that have appeared through charring. The whiskey then starts extracting chemicals from the wood that helps to develop its flavour. However, if it is left too long the flavour of the whiskey will suffer and it will take on a very woody, vanilla character.

Old whiskey does not guarantee quality. Part of the art of making whiskey is selecting casks to be used when they are peak condition. In exceptional cases in Scotland that could be after 30 to 40 years. In Ireland it is rarely beyond 20.

But no matter how good all these whiskeys are, be they pot still, single malt or grain, they could all easily be wasted if the final and most important stage is not carried out correctly: the blending. At Bushmills and Cooley the blends are made from a single malt whiskey and grain whiskey. At Midleton, Barry Walsh has a myriad of choices available and the character make-up of every whiskey is determined by a formula of ages and wood-types for every brand. Even the single malts and pure pot still have to be blended in a sense: this is called 'vatting' which is the mixing together of whiskeys from the same distillery. In contrast Frank McHardy at Bushmills knows exactly how much 10-year-old malt whiskey he requires from sherry casks and how much 11-year-old from bourbon cask, and so on.

In Scotland, the constituent whiskies of some blends are 'married' together for anything up to six months by dumping the contents of the casks into large troughs and then pumping the whisky into enormous holding vats. The idea in Scotland is that the many different types of malt and grain then get the chance to fuse or 'marry'. Single malts are sometimes treated similarly to allow the distillate from sherry and bourbon casks to find a level ground. This is not the case in Ireland. For big brands like Jameson, Powers and Paddy, the casks will be vatted together for two days, perhaps three at the most. It is only with highly specialised whiskeys like Jameson 1780, Distillery Reserve, Midleton Very Rare and the incomparable Redbreast that the constituent whiskeys may have been vatted for a full month before bottling.

But you should always remember this: no matter what the label on any bottle tells you, whiskeys never remain exactly the same — it is simply impossible. The marketing people in Scotland and Ireland may want you to think that, but the people involved in the day to day making of whiskey know better. Whiskeys mature slightly differently in different casks; temperatures of warehouses fluctuate over the seasons and there might be a slight variance in the malt used or the time taken to distil and so on. Whiskeys all have unmistakable characters, but they are *never* exactly the same. So although a vatting for Hewitt's may be exactly identical each time in terms of the choice of wood, the age of the malts and grains chosen, a vatting made six months afterwards may be a tad sweeter, a fraction maltier, a degree spicier.

This, in essence, is the most fascinating of mysteries which makes Irish whiskey so very special.

AN A-Z OF
IRISH WHISKEY

BUENA VISTA

Brand History

When American journalist Stan Delaplane stopped off at Shannon Airport on the west coast of Ireland on a return journey home, the bartender who prepared him an Irish Coffee to keep out the cold had little idea that he was to become a trendsetter. Delaplane was so impressed with this comforting concoction that he passed on the recipe to the bartender at his down-town haunt, the Buena Vista Cafe, in San Francisco.

That was in 1952 and over 40 years later no other place in the whole of America turns out Irish Coffee in the quantity of the now famous California cafe at

Fisherman's Wharf. To cope with incredible demand the management of Buena Vista struck a deal with Irish Distillers soon after the 1966 merger to supply an Irish whiskey to their own precise requirements.

They still do, with the Transatlantic traffic amounting to some 3000 cases a year. It is the only blended whiskey supplied on an exclusive basis by Irish distillers to anyone in the world.

As it was designed for Irish Coffee, like Dunphys and the now obsolete Murphys, which were sold in the States for the same purpose, it is extremely light in character; a very close relation to Tullamore Dew in style but a tad heavier on the malt and pot still. It is for sale only at the Buena Vista Cafe, but if you don't want it in your coffee, $18.75 will persuade them to allow you to take a bottle home for a closer inspection of the world's most unique Irish blend.

Tasting Notes

Nose   Despite the grain which springs to the fore, there is an almost sophisticated pot still weightiness which also adds a distinct, honeyed sweetness.

Taste   Very soft and honeyed to start, in fact, very enjoyable and relaxing with the pot still holding sway in the beginning.

Finish   Quite long with the malt dissipating early on to be replaced by a bitter, but never overly-bitter graininess coupled with a chocolate-fudge creaminess. In there, somewhere, a spiciness thinks about taking off, changes its mind, and never leaves the ground.

Comment   This is supposed to be a near relation to Tullamore Dew. A comparative tasting shows Buena Vista has considerably more elegance and is not so constrained by the rigidity of the grain. They *are* closely related, but Buena Vista — although by no means the perfect whiskey for those looking for a powerful, traditional, pot still Irish character — reveals that there is a fine line between where grain dominates at the cost of all else, and where it is just held in check. This makes Buena Vista a surprisingly pleasant whiskey to be enjoyed away from the coffee cup. But be warned — always serve at warm room temperature and never cool or serve with ice when the grain ruins it. Perfect for the Californian climate.

BUSHMILLS

Distillery History

Anyone shipwrecked in the North Channel between Kintyre and Ireland will be confused if, after tramping across land looking for habitation, they come upon the proud twin pagodas of Bushmills Distillery. Bushmills looks more like a Scottish distillery than many found these days in the Highlands. Its lines are classically those of distilleries built in the boom years of Scotch whisky in the late 19th century, and are on a very grand scale.

But Bushmills is not only Irish, it is also Ulster's final bastion of whiskey production. After the distillery was destroyed by fire in 1885 the reconstructed Bushmills would not have looked out of place on Speyside or Islay. Its rebuilding gave the owners the chance to start again with state of the art design and technology and some of the specialists brought in to raise the distillery from the ashes were, indeed, from Scotland.

The history of 'Old Bushmills' begins, however, long before that great fire of November 25th, 1885. Every bottle of Bushmills sold today, irrespective of the brand, will tell you that its contents comes 'From the World's Oldest Whiskey Distillery'. The claim is based on the undisputed fact that on April 20th, 1608 a licence was granted the Chief Governor of Ireland to Sir Thomas Phillipps, King James I's Deputy for the Plantation of Ulster *'for the next seaven yeres, within the countie of Colrane, otherwise called O Cahanes countrey, or within the territorie called the Rowte, in co. Antrim, by himselfe or his servauntes, to make, drawe, and distill such and soe great quantities of aquavite, usquabagh and aqua composita, as he or his assignes shall thinke fitt; and the same to sell, vent, and dispose of to any persons, yeeldinge yerelie the somme 13s 4d ...'*

What, however, is also beyond doubt is the simple fact that the Bushmills Old Distillery Company was not formed for another 175 years by a Hugh Anderson. When, in 1891, the company advertised their new pure malt whiskey, Old Glynn Bush, they proudly displayed 1784 as their year of establishment!

Illegal distillation had been carried out on the site since at least 1743, and with little wonder. The area in which the distillery and the village-cum-town of Bushmills is situated was known as 'The Route' on account of the River Bush being forded there by the road running from the ancient Irish capital of Tara to Antrim. For that reason any illicit whiskey found a market from both locals and passing trade. Also, nearby was a copious supply of peat and, next to where the distillery is located, a stream called St Columb's Rill (so named since it was a favourite haunt of that Saint as a boy) which empties its sweet, slightly peaty water into the Bush. Then, as now, the water was perfect for the making of whiskey.

The legalised Bushmills Distillery, like so many in Ireland at that time, was not an immediate success. Not only had it to contend with illicit distillers but also five other licensed distilleries located in the area. It also needed to sell its wares in America and the West Indies to survive. For long periods it was forced to close and when a census of operating distilleries in all Ireland was conducted in 1821, Bushmills, which by this time had long passed through not only Anderson's hands, but also those of several others, was not amongst them.

But by the time Barnard visited the distillery in around 1885 things had changed dramatically for the better. Annual output was a healthy 100,000 gallons; they had formed an arrangement with local farmers to produce all the barley they needed; the whiskey was conveyed by the novel means of an electric rail-way from Bushmills to Portrush, six miles away, from where it was shipped to its principal markets all over the world. They had even set up their own head office in Belfast, complete with sampling and boardrooms.

At that time Bushmills, like all but two Irish distilleries, did not make pure malt whiskey. It made pure Irish pot still, using a mixture of malted and unmalted barley. It was probably not until they launched the Old Glynn Bush in 1891 that they tentatively entered a market which they would later so successfully dominate. Evidence suggests they first made pure malt in

OLD BUSHMILLS DISTILLERY, FROM A COMPANY BROCHURE PUBLISHED IN 1938

1887 in order to launch a special bottling to mark Queen Victoria's Diamond Jubilee ten years later, of which 10,000 cases were eventually produced. A wait of about four years before bringing Old Glynn Bush into the world sounds about right. It is, of course, possible that the distillery became an all-malt affair when it was rebuilt in 1885, making Old Glynn a smoother 6-year-old. For reasons you will later discover, we shall never know for certain.

However, the turning point of the company's fortunes had been the buying of the distillery on August 20th, 1860 for £500 by Ballymoney spirit merchant James McColgan and one Patrick Corrigan, who was to die just five years later. With Corrigan's widow, Ellen, McColgan set about securing the future of a distillery which was lucky to have survived a prolonged period of poor trading. In 1880 they formed the distillery into a limited liability company. Under McColgan's leadership its fame grew around the world and the first of a number of gold medals were won at exhibitions in Europe, the USA, Australia and South Africa.

Even so, the distillery had a chequered career. In 1891 the company was reformed with the Mayor of Belfast, Charles Connor, and James Boyd taking control, but by 1895 it was in liquidation. It was reformed in August 1896, this time as The Old Bushmills Distillery Co. Ltd, the name it still carries today. However, by 1921 the company was again in the hands of the receivers.

It took the wily business know-how of another Boyd, almost certainly unrelated, to finally get Old Bushmills not only up and running again, but set on a course for long term success. He was a remarkable man by the name of Samuel Boyd, a Belfast wine and spirit merchant. He had been operating since before the First World War and was wealthy enough to buy Old Bushmills when it became available again in about 1923. It was seven years, though, before he registered it as a limited liability company, by which time Old Bushmills was in sound condition. Oddly, Old Bushmills had been saved not only by a devout Presbyterian, but also by a man who was given to writing temperance pamphlets, despite the fact his vast wealth had been borne on the back of alcohol. Boyd died in 1932 and the distillery continued to prosper in his family's hands and was conveniently helped by the Repeal of Prohibition in America the following year.

Expansion followed which also meant acquisition and in 1933 they bought Ireland's original malt distillery, Coleraine, and in 1936, a second, much smaller, distillery in the same town, Killowen. In 1941, fate at last caught up with the charmed life of the company records which had survived the all-consuming fire of 1885 having just been moved to the new Belfast headquarters. During one of the numerous raids on Belfast docks by German bombers, the Hill Street offices took a direct hit and all the company's documents and painstakingly detailed ledgers were lost. Fortunately, no lives were and Old Bushmills carried on regardless, despite the fact that a lot of whiskey, as well as the bottling plant, had also been lost in spectacular fashion when the Gordon Street bonds were set ablaze.

The shortage of whiskey meant that although postwar trading would be difficult and funds low, existing stocks were by then worth their weight in gold. It left the company ripe for takeover, and this followed in 1946 when Isaac Wolfson, the textile magnate who owned Great Universal Stores took control. He allowed the Boyds, with their great knowledge of the business, to continue to run the show as Wolfson used his financial clout to establish Bushmills in faraway countries of which the Boyds had once only dreamed.

In 1964 the ownership of Bushmills changed hands again. This time the move made even better commercial sense. Great Universal had not otherwise been involved in the drinks trade, but the new masters, Charringtons, were long-established in the business. With the London-based brewers owning 5,000 pubs and 650 off-licences, the distillery had a captive market. One of their first moves was to bring all the bottling from Coleraine to Bushmills and develop a new blending area. Bushmills was becoming self-sufficient.

By the time the last of the Boyds had retired from the Bushmills board in 1973, the distillery had again changed hands. Once more the step was in an upward direction with the giant Canadian distillers Seagrams taking it under their wing. Bushmills had remained the last distillery in Ireland to stay outside the Irish Distillers Group when that was formed in 1966. However, Irish Distillers bought Bushmills shares from Seagrams and the result was that by 1972 IDG finally achieved overall control. And with the parent company being eventually taken over by Paris-based Pernod-Ricard, not only was the opportunity for Bushmills to further establish itself worldwide greatly enhanced, but the long-term future of the distillery finally secured beyond doubt.

BUSHMILLS 5-YEAR-OLD SINGLE MALT

Brand History

This is the youngest single whiskey bottled by Bushmills and brought out exclusively for the Italians who, for whatever reason, appear to enjoy youthful whiskey. The biggest whisky success story in Italy has been the Glen Grant 5-year-old Scotch malt and the Bushmills 5-year-old has been designed to attack the same market.

The brand has only been in Italian outlets since 1992, so these are early days to see if it will be a success. But because Bushmills does produce a rather light whiskey there are more sherry casks used in this vatting than the established 10-year-old.

Tasting Notes

Nose   Raw, citrousy and youthful. The malt is very clean indeed, but it is really light.

Taste   Quite fat on the mouth, oily and very beautifully malty. There is an unmistakably sweet maltiness which sets Bushmills apart from everything else at any age, and it is here in abundance.

Finish   Piles of vanilla and all things bourbon cask, including chocolate and spice. Some very shy sherry notes also float about at the finish.

Comment A quite different character to the Glen Grant which originally set the 5-year-old trend in Italy, since this is softer and oilier. For its tender age, though, it does have a surprising depth, and it is surprisingly enjoyable. I didn't expect this. I have been able to taste this at cask strength before being reduced and it is then absolutely superb. They should really think about releasing that too!

BUSHMILLS 10-YEAR-OLD SINGLE MALT

Brand History

During the long hot summer of 1984, Bushmills Distillery unwittingly turned full circle. It had just launched its first pure malt whiskey since the Second World War and it was approaching its centenary since changing codes from a pot still to an all-malt distillery.

Bushmills 10-year-old was first offered to the home Irish market but since then its exposure has grown considerably.

Now commonly found on supermarket shelves throughout the United Kingdom, it is accepted as one of the most recognised faces of Irish whiskey. In 1993 it was introduced into the USA for the first time where Original Bushmills, or White Bush, had been a favourite for many years.

The whiskeys used in the vatting of this single malt range from ten to 12 years, with the occasional batch of 13-year-old casks being added for good measure. Being a light malt, only a little new sherry wood is used in maturation, but it is certainly enough to give it a fruity feel.

Tasting Notes

Nose   Rather too light and spirity when cold but once warmed in the hand, whilst remaining light, it becomes an altogether maltier whiskey with a hint of sherry. Oddly, despite being all malt, it does have a pot still brittleness to it which gives it a discernibly Irish edge.

Taste   A sweet start with even a gentle fruitiness. But the middle is emphatically malt and the sweet richness, helped out by some sherry cask, is gradually replaced by a more austere dryness.

Finish   Quite long with lots of malt and toffee and a pleasant spiciness. A chocolate-vanilla feel also enters the fray from the use of ex-bourbon casks which makes for an essentially dry finish with a rumbling bitterness in the background.

Comment   This is a very pleasant malt: simple, untaxing and slightly fuller-bodied than of old. It is also a rather lazy malt which resists asserting itself on the tastebuds as its original bright start suggests it might. Still ... very refreshing, quaffable and moreish, nonetheless.

BUSHMILLS MILLENNIUM

Brand History

The ultimate Irish whiskey? Perhaps. Those of you with several thousand pounds to spare will find out in the year 2000 when this 25-year-old whiskey will finally be bottled in time for the world's biggest party.

It's not a unique idea since Bushmills corporate sister distillery in Scotland, Aberlour, is doing something along the same lines. Also, an 8-year-old single malt made from purely organic grain will be available by the cask from Springbank, Campbeltown. So Bushmills Millennium is Ireland's contribution.

The casks currently maturing are ex-sherry, but for the last few years before the big day, the whiskey will be finished in bourbon casks so as to make sure the sherry does not dominate too much; 25 years is a long time for a malt as light as Bushmills. Each cask is expected to provide a minimum 250 bottles at 70cl or 228 bottles at 75cl, depending which side of the Atlantic the buyer comes from. The labels will also carry the respective purchaser's name.

A nice touch, if you can afford it.

Tasting Notes

(Distilled 1975, sample tasted July 1994.)

Nose	Very confident and forceful; nowhere near the amount of sherry one would have expected and little sign of wear and tear. The maltiness holds up well alongside the fruit and although by no means complex, it is very much alive and well.
Taste	At cask strength the sherried-fruitiness is first to show, being quite sweet and raisiny. As this dies down it is content to share the middle with the malt which begins to show strongly after a quiet start, finally passing the winner's post while leading.
Finish	Very malty with just the first signs of a

wood presence, which is not in the least bit sappy. Some sherry notes linger alongside a gentle, gingery, spice with a vanilla topping to finish it all off.

Comment Quite delicious at this stage and holding up to the years very well indeed. Bushmills at cask strength does have an extra edge that the normal bottling misses somewhat and it's not just because of the extra alcohol content. The malt does become rather more than two dimensional. My biggest surprise is the lack of sherry influence.

BUSHMILLS ORIGINAL

Brand History

No one knows just how long White Bush, as it is affectionately known, has been on the market. Those records were lost when the Bushmills offices were razed in the last war. Equally, there is confusion as to whether it began life as a single malt, or as a blend since Bushmills did not have access to their own grain whiskey until the 1950s. Certainly it is accepted that by the end of the Second World War, it was a blend which did exceptionally well on the export market.

Even today White Bush remains the best known of Bushmills brands and it is the lightest in character bearing the Bushmills name. The malt used in the blending is unlikely to be more than six years old and the grain whiskey only half that age. It has been designed to combat ordinary Scottish blends, so its malt/grain ratio will reflect that, with only about a third consisting of malt.

Tasting Notes

Nose Massive grain presence and little discernible malt. Some sherry does show though.

Taste Soft and smooth in the extreme and very sweet. But any palate on the lookout for a malty cushion will be disappointed. It does filter through at the beginning and traces still hang around for the thin middle.

Finish   The grain now comes back with a vengeance. Any balance there might have been at the start is wiped out at the end as it becomes bitter rather lacking in style. However, a pleasant sweetness does follow through.

Comment   This, I'm afraid, is not my cup of tea, or glass of whiskey, come to that. Far too simplistic, grain-dominated and hardly one for the connoisseur. The finish in particular needs some attention. But having said that, I have a couple of friends who drink nothing else — one of them insists on taking it with ice! And it *is* a big seller. So what do I know?

BUSHMILLS BLACK BUSH

Brand History

As in the case of White Bush, no one has been able to come up with a date of establishment for this most noble of Irish blends. It started life as Bushmills Liqueur Whiskey, designed to be heavy in character to counterbalance the lightness of White Bush. But because of the dark label the customers christened it Black Bush and the name stuck. However, it only enjoyed moderate success in Ireland until the 1960s when a shortage of older stocks of malt meant that it was almost impossible to find in the bars.

A cry went up amongst its regular drinkers and, human nature being what it is, those who hadn't normally drunk it started asking for it and others who had never tasted it at all wanted to know what all the fuss was about. The rest, as they say, is history.

Bushmills is easily regarded as the finest blend amongst drinkers in the North and has a massive following outside Ireland. That is hardly surprising since it has a malt content of around 75%, most of which is eight years old with the grain being only a couple of years younger.

Tasting Notes

Nose This nose is nothing less than a classic. It has absolutely everything: exceptionally well-defined malt, gentle sherry notes, high quality grain softness and, dare I say it, a touch of peat in there as well. Not only does it have everything, but like the best things in life, they are all in the right proportion too.

Taste As this whiskey melts in your mouth, you melt into your chair. Very full-bodied and malt-rich with a fine sherry background. Again there is a peaty tune being played somewhere and as the malt-sherry middle fades, a superb spiciness develops.

Finish Initially spicy, then dampens down to become sweetish with a pleasant sherry cask/bourbon cask conflict going on between the respective woods. Like the nose and palate, it's never dull and always of the very highest quality.

Comment Some years back I regarded this as probably the finest blend in either Scotland or Ireland. My allegiance has shifted in recent years to Powers, but this is nothing less than a beautifully crafted whiskey which retains a delightful silkiness despite the complexity of all that is going on. An absolute stunner.

43

BUSHMILLS 1608

Brand History

This was the first Irish whiskey designed exclusively for the duty-free market and there is no problem determining the origin of this brand. Launched in October 1992 the idea was to offer an Irish whiskey with a degree of exclusivity. Even if you visit the distillery, you won't be able to buy it there.

A pity. This is too good a blend for Irish whiskey lovers to miss out on. But the distillers say that they have insufficient stocks of what goes to make this brand to enable them to cater for anything other than the target market.

There is hardly any grain in this blend, perhaps around 10%, making this a real top-of-the-range job. The malts used are usually 12 years old although some 14-year-old may sneak in and the grain is a minimum of 12 years old as well. A good cross-section of wood here; a lot of sherry and the ex-bourbon carrying the grain helps give the blend its distinctive spiciness.

Originally only sold in litre bottles, miniatures are now available, but, tantalisingly, only from duty-free.

Tasting Notes

Nose   The moment you put a glass of 1608 to
            your nose, you know you are in the com-
            pany of a cracker. Malt, sherry and spice
            all come together in equal measure, each
            intermingling in a truly astonishing com-
            plexity. But that's not all: there are even
            the faintest traces of pine, mint and honey.

Taste   The palate is immediately held in the grip
            of a spicy attack which takes you by sur-
            prise. Acting as a buffer is a silky honey-
            rich maltiness with clean sherry notes also
            adding to the fun. The sum total is a mas-
            sive assertiveness in the mouth.

Finish   Perhaps the only disappointment with this
            blend. It dies away rather too quickly, some
            caramel notes being left behind. So, too,
            are gentle spices. Maybe a shade too bit-
            ter and metallic in the grand finale, though.

Comment   This is one of Ireland's best whiskeys with
            a complex dovetailing of a great many fea-
            tures on the nose and palate. A very confi-
            dent whiskey with one of the most luxuri-
            ous mouth-feels of any whiskey in the
            world. Beautiful.

BUSHMILLS 14-YEAR-OLD SINGLE MALT

Tasting Notes

From Wm Cadenhead 1977 Distillation 60.6% abv

Nose A very fruity Irish whiskey indeed. Sharp spirit and an odd ammonia effect does bite a little, but beyond that and the malt, can be located some citric notes.

Taste Extremely lively on the palate, always remaining very light. Starts slightly creamy, then intensifies to malt. The middle is a powerful meeting of malt and woody notes.

Finish The wood does have a strong say here. The effect, therefore, is dry, though never bitter. The malt comes through rather as burnt toffee and some woody oiliness clings about as well.

Comment The nose is quite unforgiving, but to taste this is a real mixed bag of tricks. Much better on the second glass when you've had a chance to get used to it. Even in this form there remains something more Irish than Scottish about this malt. Quite delicious in places, this whiskey will shock those used to Bushmills in its more inert, distillery bottled, form.

BUSHMILLS 16-YEAR-OLD SINGLE MALT

ESTABLISHED 1842

CADENHEAD'S
Authentic
Collection

from
OLD BUSHMILLS
D I S T I L L E R Y
Matured in an Oak Cask
FOR **16** YEARS
Distilled May 1977
BOTTLED ON ST. PATRICK'S DAY MARCH 17 1994

70 cl   58.4% vol

Cask
Strength
SINGLE MALT
IRISH WHISKEY

BOTTLED BY
WM. CADENHEAD 32 UNION STREET CAMPBELTOWN SCOTLAND

Tasting Notes

From Wm Cadenhead 1977 distillation 58.4% abv

Nose   Much kinder and more easily enjoyed than the previous bottling. The slightly offensive vapours have died down to reveal a quite relaxed, sweet, easy-going and even slightly honeyed nose.

Taste   Wow! Although lessened in alcoholic strength, in terms of taste power this does take some holding. That first oily-creaminess starts it all off and then there is a malty fruitiness which is quite sweet in places. But the wood takes far more time to come through and the middle holds for much

47

longer with a more full-bodied confidence.

Finish The finish has vanilla toffee and some roast coffee tones running through it. Very long and quite superb.

Comment One can only assume that the cask in which this Bushmills was matured was a lot better than the previous bottling. This is absolute nectar from beginning to end, affording a balance found nowhere in the 14-year-old and a complexity beyond any Bushmills (at cask strength or from the distillery bottling) I have ever experienced before. In this form it single-handedly destroys those who claim Bushmills is incapable of producing exceptional whiskey. Brilliant.

COLERAINE

Distillery History

While Bushmills is today known the world over for its single malt Irish whiskey, a century ago it was Coleraine which enjoyed that honour. Only the Waterside Distillery in Derry also made pure malt whiskey and although its output was twice that of Coleraine, it was held in only half the esteem.

Today, however, Coleraine is just one of a number of Irish distilleries of which little is left intact, having been bought out, swallowed up and then closed. When it was in operation until the 1960s, Coleraine, had it so wanted, could have shared Bushmills' ambitious claim to being the oldest licensed distillery in the world, since the licence granted to Bushmills in 1608 applied equally to the district around Coleraine. But whereas Bushmills, as a company, wasn't formed until 1784, Coleraine came on the scene somewhat later. The building apparently began life as a flour mill, which may account for the murals of sheaves which can still be seen woven into part of the remaining structure which was not converted into a distillery until 1820.

While many distilleries struggled to keep going at this time, there was no such problem for Coleraine. By 1845 it was already on sale in the bars of the House of Commons and because of this honour the distillers marketed their malt as Old Irish HC Whisky (always without the 'e'.)

The man who originally supplied it was James Moore who had bought the distillery some time earlier. Moore was a proven distiller, already owning Bann Distillery, and a maltman to boot, so the company was quite well established by the time Robert Taylor, a local dignitary, acquired the distillery in 1869 following Moore's death. It was both rather fitting and also ironic that the distillery bearing the HC logo should pass into the Taylor family's hands, because five years later his brother Daniel became Liberal MP for Coleraine and he was a noted sympathiser of the Temperance movement.

Robert Taylor, who had been a partner in his family's grocery business, showed he was not taking his new profession lightly. As well as the distillery he also ensured that he secured all the stocks of Coleraine whiskey held in bond not only at the distillery, but also in Belfast and Ballymena.

The reputation of the distillery continued, like its business, to flourish. Between them Taylor and distillery manager Edward Reid made not only one of the most prized malts in Britain, but did so in a distillery which amazed all those who visited it. Among them was Alfred Barnard, coming to the end of his tour of Ireland, who was unusually moved to remark: 'In all our wanderings through Erin's Green Isle, for cleanliness, order and regularity, we have seen no distillery to beat this. The Stillmen seem to take a pride and delight in their work and regard these old Pot Stills with veneration.'

Oddly, in an age when distillers and brewers set out to collect as many gold medals as they could at exhibitions, Coleraine was laid back about collecting gongs: it felt confident enough about its product. The only one it did enter was the Edinburgh Exhibition in 1886. It won!

In 1899 Robert Taylor was knighted. He had long been a JP and legend has it that when he had the one-legged 'Stamper' Thompson up before him on a charge of being drunk and disorderly 'Stamper', well known locally as something of a poet, rasped in reply to how he was to plead:

Vance Macauley grew the barley,
Robert Taylor brewed the Malt,
Stamper Thompson drank the whiskey
So who the devil is at fault?

After Robert Taylor's death in 1902, the distillery fell into steady decline. It had been taken over by his nephew, Andrew Clarke, but Coleraine under his auspices failed to maintain the high standing it had gained under his uncle's reign. Production ceased in the early 1920s and the distillery remained silent until the late '30's, by which time it had been bought by the Boyd's, owners of Bushmills.

Although the purchase was made in 1933, it wasn't until 1938 that the Boyds began making malt whiskey there again. But the stills hissed for only a short time before the Second World War, and the shortages of barley which that brought meant it had to close down again.

When peace was won, Coleraine again reopened its doors, not only as a distillery but also as the bottling hall for both distilleries. With the move towards blended whiskey Coleraine was also selected as the distillery to house patent stills to produce grain whiskey alongside its famous malt.

But with cost-cutting in operation in March 1964, just two months before Great Universal Stores sold the Bushmills Company to Charrington's, and with it Coleraine, the last-ever malt whiskey from this most famous of distilleries was squeezed from the stills. It continued until 1978 as a grain plant but then that arm of the operation was closed down since a similar style grain was by then being produced at Midleton.

Found right in the town centre, parts of the old distillery can still be seen today (the warehouses are being demolished as I write), though a block of flats and a nightclub stand on the greater part of the site. To the last, the quality of Coleraine pure single malt whiskey remained wonderfully high. Its closure was a sad loss, not only for distilling in Ulster, but for the Irish whiskey industry in general.

COLERAINE BLEND

Finest Quality

COLERAINE

ESTABLISHED 1825

irish whiskey

DISTILLED
BLENDED AND BOTTLED BY
THE OLD BUSHMILLS DISTILLERY CO. LTD.
BUSHMILLS CO. ANTRIM

40% vol   PRODUCE OF IRELAND   700 ml e

Brand History

The most parochial of all Bushmills whiskeys, this one keeps its fans happy in the northernmost part of Ulster. Only 10,000 cases are produced each year, but that may begin to rise if it continues to improve from the mind-numbingly bland whiskey it used to be.

Many hotels and bars I've visited have a bottle around somewhere and its very light style means that it also appears in the local retail outlets alongside other cheaper blends.

Launched to keep the old distillery name alive, it barely does justice to it although I've always understood there to be roughly equal portions of grain to malt. Just like White Bush, the malt used has been aged about six years and the grain is somewhere around four. It is virtually impossible to find anywhere outside Ulster.

Tasting Notes

Nose
Uncompromising grain whiskey dominance, and pretty young grains at that. There is a musty maltiness alongside caramel, but it's all too sweet and murky to make any sense out of it.

Taste
Soft and yielding on the palate, the malt flits across the taste buds rather quickly allowing the grain to dominate. There is also some spice around that hasn't been sensed in previous years.

Finish
Quite an attractive, well-balanced and rather moreish finish. The malt returns rather superficially but the grain has very pleasant bourbon wood notes and sweet cream-caramel toffee, all of which adds character.

Comment
This whiskey has improved out of all recognition from a few years back. Then it was an unsophisticated and bland whiskey in the extreme with a redeeming and mystifying Irish pot still fruitiness. More recent bottlings have been considerably better structured with the malt having a far greater say at the expense of a grain which had little going for it. By strange coincidence, the introduction of the caramel notes, which I've never noticed before, has arrived at the same time as a marked deepening of the whiskey's colour. Can that by any way be related? Worth trying these days, anyway.

COLERAINE 34-YEAR-OLD SINGLE MALT

Brand History

To a romantic such as myself there is an acute sense of sadness when an era comes to an end for something as wonderful as Coleraine Distillery.

Over the years Bushmills hung on to some Coleraine casks from the now demolished mecca of Irish malt, but there came a time when something had to be done. If you leave whiskey in wood for ever it will ruin; whiskey matures only in the cask, never in the glass.

A sample was drawn and everyone agreed that the whiskey tasted wonderful. But what would it be like in a year's time? To my mind the management at Bushmills made exactly the right decision: they decided to bottle.

A 34-year wait in the cask was over. It had been distilled and filled into cask on March 19th, 1959. On June 7th, 1993, the cask was emptied, still boasting a strength of 57.1% abv so there was enough whiskey to fill 396 individually numbered bottles. These went on sale at £300 apiece and within nine months only around 100 remained unsold. It is highly unlikely that will be the case when the next edition of this book is produced but there will be 396 content whiskey lovers keeping the spirit of Coleraine alive around the world. And, yes, you've guessed: I'll be one of the privileged few.

Tasting Notes

Nose   Quite glorious in its extraordinary intensity; definite traces of wood but these only add to the depth and pungency. The malt is very fine, clean and sweet yet still there is that peculiar, oily Irishness about it.

Taste   The malt tones are truly superb, slowly strolling from sweet honey to dry. But never, never, allowing the wood presence to dominate.

Finish   Deep with a bourbony-liquorice. All the time the malt makes its presence felt and even at the very last some heather-honey notes refuse to die. Outstanding.

Comment This is a proud old-timer, a full-bodied ghost of one of Ireland's greatest-ever distilleries. Just as well they bottled it when they did, since another summer in the wood might have tipped the balance. As it is, this is something special to remember this wonderful distillery by. The big question is: do you keep it for posterity, or drink it?

OLD COMBER PURE POT STILL

Distillery History

It is hard to imagine Northern Ireland having a dozen working distilleries less than 70 years ago. Yet that was the case, and although that was two fewer than the Irish Free State, their combined output was twice as much.

In Eire it was the smaller distilleries which withered and died; in Northern Ireland exactly the reverse happened. By 1953 Ulster's three smallest distilleries, Comber, Coleraine and Bushmills were all that was left of a proud distilling tradition. By the end of the year the number was down to two.

The demise of Comber in the February of Coronation year was a sad landmark in Irish distilling history. The silencing of the stills saw the end of the making of pot still whiskey in Ulster: Bushmills and Coleraine made malt or grain only.

The distillery's earliest years were curious. There were two Comber distilleries located in that small town close to Belfast. They were called the Upper and Lower Distilleries, and it was the former which was the senior in standing. In some respects the distilleries were twins: they were both established in 1825, though quite independently, by being converted from buildings serving different purposes.

The Upper Distillery began life as a brewery and malthouse before Johnston & Miller invested the £8,000 required to alter the output from beer to whiskey. Down the road Byrne & Giffikin turned a paper mill into the Lower Distillery but some 20 years later John Miller bought out the smaller distillery and ran the two plants simultaneously.

Alfred Barnard did not find either particularly interesting, and obviously having an off day and weary from his daily grind of surveying Britain's distilleries to the smallest detail, summed up the two Combers in the briefest terms. Instead, he found the journey to the distillery much more exciting: 'We left the Royal Avenue Hotel in a very tipsy-looking jaunting car, with a driver to match the vehicle. His coat had evidently been handed down from a past generation, its skirts touching his heels, whilst his battered white hat and his knee-breeches were of like ancient date. He assured us on his honour that he would catch the Comber train; he kept his word, but it was at the peril of our lives. He bowled us along almost upsetting us at every corner, we collided with other vehicles, almost ran over one old woman and three street urchins, and we inwardly vowed we would never again let a jarvey know that we were in a hurry.'

The Comber Distilleries' Company may have been among the first Irish distillers to pioneer bottled whiskey, but the relatively heavy, pure, pot still they produced began to lose ground in the markets against lighter, blended whiskies. So the company's decline and fall, especially during and after the Second World War, was classic by Irish standards. And it sadly reinforced the fact that reputation, of which Comber always enjoyed the very highest, counted for nothing in the harsh climate of commerce.

Brand History

By the time the Ulster-based wine merchants and distillers' agents, James E. McCabe, managed to get hold of Comber Distilleries, there was little to salvage.

For 17 years the company had beeen picked clean, first by H.D. Wines of Inverness who had bought it after closure. They did a roaring trade out of the scrap and some of the remaining whiskey stocks. Four years later, in 1957, two gentlemen called Hollywood and Donnelly bought what remained, sold off even more whiskey until finally, in 1970, McCabe took over.

They set about buying up as much old stock of Comber as they could find throughout Ireland's bonded warehouses. But it never amounted to very much.

In the early 1980s they launched a brand called Old Comber, bottling the whiskey before the wood did irreparable damage to it. It was at least 30 years old and since then less than a few hundred bottles have been sold each year, mainly in Northern Ireland.

Stocks are now very low. In fact three years ago I was told by whiskey merchants in the north that the very last drop of Old Comber had long since been drunk. But during the course of researching this book I discovered there are still a couple of hundred bottles still in bond. Not for very much longer, I suspect.

COMBER DISTILLERIES CO. LTD.

Est^d 1825

TRADE MARK

AT LEAST 30 YEARS OLD

OLD COMBER
IRISH WHISKEY

GUARANTEED
PURE POT STILL

PRODUCE OF IRELAND

40% VOL.
75cl.

DISTILLED AND BOTTLED FOR
COMBER DISTILLERIES COMPANY LTD COMBER IRELAND

70°
PROOF

Tasting Notes

Nose   A glorious and quite unique combination of pure honey and pot still. Very sweet with definite traces of malt with the pot still not being hidden by anything like the amount of wood one would expect from a 30-year-old Irish whiskey. There is an unmistakable resiny presence, nontheless.

Taste   Begins with a soft, breezy maltiness which is attractive for its gentleness. But this is cut rather abruptly short by a wood surge totally out of proportion with the nose. This means the middle is almost non-existent. Yet before the wood arrives one is aware of a strange mint/menthol coolness which combines with an almost cameo pot still appearance.

Finish   Rather disappointing, to be honest. The wood takes too firm a grip, with the sappy bitterness refusing to allow the sweet honey tones that had been so prevalent earlier to get a look in. It does settle down towards the very end with that mint/menthol freshness returning and, thankfully, a defiant pot still hardness reminding us, all too briefly, of former glory days.

Comment   A truly classic example of a whiskey that has spent too long in the wood: increasing age does not equal increasing excellence. Despite this it is drinkable but you are always thinking of how very good this might have at only half its age. Having said that, if you are lucky enough to spot Old Comber, buy it, for this really is one for the collector. An absolute must for the serious Irish whiskey connoisseur, and if you must open the bottle then just savour that voluptuously beautiful nose.

DUNPHYS

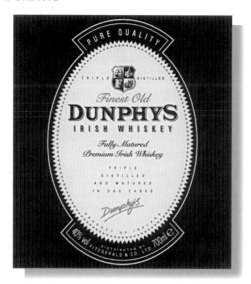

Brand History

Few whiskeys have a more curious history than Dunphys. In effect it was an Irish whiskey to be drunk anything but straight. The 1950s saw Irish whiskey enjoy a mini-boom in the United States for the most unlikely of reasons. A modest craze swept the nation: the drinking of Irish coffee. To fan the flames of this craze it was thought a good idea to produce as cheap an Irish whiskey as possible which people would buy especially for that purpose, while they could keep their better, more expensive brands safely in their cocktail cabinets for more serious drinking.

It was decided to create a whiskey which was light in nature, so a blend was produced, made by Cork Distilleries in tandem some American distillers. To keep the price down further the whiskey was shipped out to the USA in bulk and bottled there.

Although the boom, like all fashionable things,

peaked and then subsided, Dunphys could still be found in the USA until 1988, when it was withdrawn as part of Irish Distillers' masterplan to concentrate purely on the Jameson and Bushmills brands.

But Dunphys lives on in the Irish Republic, a young blend of high grain content fighting it out on the market shelf against the cheaper downmarket Scotches.

Tasting Notes

Nose The grain takes solid control here; nowhere near enough malt or pot still balance. Also some odd creosote and tarry notes which spice it up. A hint of sweetness in there, but not enough to create a balance.

Taste The grain is evident in a somewhat brutal manner, taking no prisoners and making little attempt to charm. Some pot still filters through on the third wave which crashes against the palate, but even this is a rather sorry attempt at achieving some egality.

Finish Usually, a long finish suggests a classy whiskey. This is the exception. Dunphy is the most bitter and unpleasant of any Irish I can think of. The bitterness seems to go back to that tar and creosote: it's all-consuming and no attractive points manage to battle through. The grain refuses to yield whatsoever.

Comment When you arrive in Ireland and at last taste a whiskey you have long looked forward to getting to know, it is a terrible disappointment when it turns out like this. From the nose through to the finish there is little if any balance or style. The grain is not only dominant, but appears to be of a strain which is quite charmless. Keep it in the coffee cup!

GREEN SPOT PURE POT STILL

GREEN SPOT

IRISH WHISKEY

700 ml ℮   40% vol.

MITCHELL & SON

Distilled, matured and bottled for
Mitchell & Son Limited, 21 Kildare Street, Dublin 2.
PRODUCT OF IRELAND

Brand History

Green Spot is to the true Irish whiskey drinker what
an Irish Round Tower is to the archaeologist. It is a
beautifully preserved, almost living, throwback to the
old Ireland which takes some searching to locate, but
once found, is an experience to savour. When I first
discovered it in a shop in Galway, it was like finding
the pot of gold at the end of the rainbow.

Once upon a time in Ireland, many hundreds of
wine merchants would fill their own casks with the
spirit from their local distilleries and sell it under their
own name, occasionally giving mention to the stills
where it first bubbled into life. But all that changed
when distillers became proprietorial and wished, often with good reason due to the dubious practices of
some merchants, to have complete control over any
whiskey which bore their name. As businesses closed
or merged, brands were lost. Others decided not to
compete with the ever more powerful distillers. Sometimes distillers simply refused to supply the whiskey.

In the end, there was only one left which can still be found today. That sole surviver is Green Spot. There are no exact records as to when the brand first hit the streets, but certainly by the early 1920s the long-established wine merchants of Mitchell & Son of Kildare Street, Dublin, were annually putting to one side 100 sherry hogsheads to be filled at Jameson's Bow Street distillery.

So that the whiskey was not too overpowered by the wine, half of the casks used had held oloroso and other dark sherries, while the other half were the former homes of lighter finos. The Jameson pot still whiskey would mature for five years in those casks before being vatted together and then allowed to blend and mature for a further five years in those same butts in Mitchell's old bonded warehouses in Fitzwilliam Lane.

At first the brand was called Pat Whisky, with a man looking very much the worse for wear apparently bursting through the label. Behind him was green shading. From this grew the name Green Spot. The popularity of the whiskey spread to a seven-year-old Blue Spot, a Yellow Spot (12) and Red Spot (15).

As the costs involved in maturing expensive sherry casks became heavier and heavier, Mitchell reverted to vatting just the single and original Green version. However, when Jameson switched production from Bow Street to John's Lane the make-up of the whisky altered for the first time in living memory. Mitchell's maturing stocks were running low and, having no intention of losing their famous brand, the company entered into a contractual agreement with Irish Distillers for them to continue to produce the whiskey. A stipulation was that the whiskey supplied had to be matured in Midleton's own casks, but IDG were able to guarantee the future of the brand as pure single pot still whiskey.

The current Green Spot is made entirely from seven and eight-year-old Midleton pot still, a healthy 25% coming from sherry cask, which is quite evident in its aroma and taste. With Irish Distillers producing their own 12-year-old pot still, Redbreast, it was understandable they were not willing to produce an older vatting for Mitchell's. But when Redbreast was taken off the market, Green Spot enjoyed the distinction of being the only, and very last, pure Irish pot still whiskey commercially produced, with Old Comber relying on ancient stocks. Now with Midleton back on the shelves it can no longer claim that, but it does remain the longest running pot still whiskey to be continuously produced in the Republic.

Only 500 cases are made up each year, all for the home market. Those meagre 6000 bottles represent only a very small part of the Mitchell wine and spirit operation. But for a family company which dates back to 1805, it is one they cherish as a vital part of their own history and Ireland's whiskey heritage.

Tasting Notes

Nose   The first thing to strike you is the density of the nose — nothing light and flowery here. The pot still appears older than its eight years thanks to a pleasant dustiness (something similar to old Redbreast), and the influence of the sherry. All this is mixed with a curious menthol sub-stratum. Some evidence of bourbon wood around, too, but rather overshadowed by this highly unusual cough-sweet malty effect.

Taste   Sweet, rich and full-bodied from the very start. It quickly fills the mouth with a glorious spiciness. All the time it somehow remains soft, though the tastebuds are constantly tweaked by a harder pot still maltiness. Wonderfully complex and busy.

Finish   Very long, dry and malty to start then sweetens and some late spice adds to all the fun. The very last, dying rays are rather cool on the throat, as if the menthol on the nose has returned.

Comment   This is a tremendous whiskey, sometimes even giving a sweet-honey feel more associated with Perthshire malts from Scotland. But the pot still is confident enough to confirm this as Irish with a maturity greater than the age of the whiskey used. If you see it, grab it. It's too much of a high-class one-off to ignore.

HEWITTS

Brand History

The diversity of whiskeys produced within the Midleton Distillery is quite stunning. And with Hewitts, a whiskey of hitherto unsung beauty, we have another one-off. It is a heavier whisky than many Irish blends and that is because this is a blend of two single malts and a single grain; the only whiskey IDG market from Midleton where there is no pot still whatsoever.

To achieve a balance, it is a blend of two types of malt: one light, the other heavy. The weight of the malt produced at Midleton is often determined by which part of the run off from the still, called the cut, is selected. To produce a lighter malt you narrow the cut from the very heart of the run. The more feints and foreshots you use, the heavier and oilier the spirit, and thus the whiskey, becomes. The overall heaviness is further compounded by the amount of feints and foreshots from the previous distillation put through the still. Whatever the case here, the vatted malt which goes into Hewitts from Midleton is heavier and more full-bodied than the malt from Bushmills which is also used in this brand. It is also deceptive in that the whiskeys used seem a lot more mature than the six to ten-year-olds actually used.

Hewitts was launched in the early 1960s purely for the home market. It was designed to do battle against Scotch and, originally, peated malt was used, though no more. Today it continues to be found only in Eire, where Munster is its heartland.

The name was chosen after a Thomas Hewitt, a merchant of Cork who, with two other businessmen, founded the Watercourse Distillery in 1782. By 1868 the distillery was wholly owned by the Hewitt family before it amalgamated that year with two of the city's other distilleries at North Mall and The Green and with Daly's of John Street, as well as the Midleton Distilllery to form the Cork Distilleries Co.

Although the Watercourse handed over the distilling reins to North Mall, it continued as a maltings and warehouse centre. In 1916 it began distilling again, only this time the output was grain whiskey. Today the remains of the distillery, including its chimney, can still be clearly seen along with most of the proud Victorian buildings, some with faded distillery lettering on them, having been turned into a small industrial estate. But sadly its days are numbered: it is due to be torn down in the very near future to make way for a new road.

Tasting Notes

Nose — I love it: not only plenty of malt, but the heavy, plummy fruitiness and the clarity of it nestles perfectly with a grain whiskey which knows when to keep its distance whilst giving a distinct Irishness. Top rate stuff, this.

Taste — This is a blend which moulds itself around your mouth. You cannot escape from a single part of its extraordinary complexity and depth. It begins with a powerful malt theme, switching to sweet honey-fruit and then a peppery spiciness. None of this is laid back: it is all very forceful and confident.

Finish — The finish dries quite dramatically by comparison to the previous sweetness. The grain comes through with a particularly woody feel and is a comparative let-down to the all-round charisma of what has gone before. Having said that, it's a long finish with some bourbony notes added in for good measure and it is never dull.

Comment If you ever see this on the shelf of a bar or store, get it. It is totally unlike any other whiskey I have ever tasted in Ireland and certainly one of the most complex. It is in some ways the least Irish of any produced by IDG: even Bushmills and its associated blends show a pot still character for some unknown reason. This doesn't and I must say on the evidence of this, I wish Irish Distillers would bottle a single malt from Midleton now that Cooley has stolen Bushmills' thunder. Wonderful.

JAMESON

CASKS ARE ROLLED ON TO JAMESON'S TRANSPORT AT THE BOW STREET DISTILLERY, CIRCA 1924

Distillery History

Just as the genesis of Irish whiskey cannot be told, lost as it is in uncharted history, it seems quite fitting that the very earliest days of the most famous name in Irish whiskey can be viewed with an equal lack of clarity. Read a different book and you will be told a different story. Whether Bow Street Distillery was founded by John Jameson or whether he took it over from others, is not at all important. What is important is the way the company became, by mid-Victorian times, not only one of the most dominant distillers in Ireland, but makers of one of the most consistently high-quality pot still spirits in the land.

When Barnard paid his visit in 1884 he was told the distillery was founded by three wealthy men including a Baronet and a General, and it was from them that the grandfather of the proprietors bought the business at the beginning of the 19th century. However, a book partly produced by Jameson's five years earlier dismissed that tale as no more than a 'tradition' and admitted: 'There is no one living who knows, and there is no discoverable documentary evidence to show, what was the date of foundation, neither can we even say at what date, prior to 1802, the distillery passed into the hands of the ancestor of the present proprietors.'

However, it appears some evidence was discovered by the company which in 1924 published a detailed history and a shorter one some 26 years later, though both offered slightly differing accounts of Jameson's earliest days. It seems that the original John Jameson was a Scotsman from Alloa who had married into the Haig distilling dynasty and who, while still in his 30s, rose to the post of Sheriff Clerk of Clackmannanshire.

A confident man, he sought his fortune in Ireland, arriving in Dublin sometime in the 1770s. His two sons, John and William, got to know a distiller by the name of John Stein who was operating in Bow Street and John, the elder of the two, then married Stein's daughter Isabella. John Jameson senior took over the Bow Street Distillery around 1780 and was later succeeded by his son John. Brother William meanwhile ran a second Stein distillery at Marrowbone Lane which was to later bear his name after he gained control. Between them John and William Jameson forged the biggest distilling family in Irish history, though the Bow Street and Marrowbone Lane distilleries were nothing less than business rivals.

There remain big question marks regarding the dates and order of things, although for over 50 years John Jameson & Son has settled upon 1780 as the year of the company's formation. Certainly by 1810 John Jameson was operating a 1256-gallon still making pot still whiskey, and when in production 11 years later, it was the second-largest in all Ireland. Strangely, the biggest of all was operated by Jameson and Dewar, doubtless another but less well-known branch of the family.

The distillery continued to prosper and was in perfect financial health to enable expansion in the latter half of the 19th century as the popularity of Irish whiskey grew worldwide. By the mid-1880s the distillery had become quite enormous. It took 300 people to run it and some 1 million gallons of spirit were produced each year. The whiskey was double-distilled in a still room boasting four enormous stills: the wash stills held 24,000 gallons each with the low wines stills holding 14,500 and 13,000 gallons respectively. Because the stills were so large, not only were they heated directly by coal fires from below, but they also used internal steam coils, a practice which was way ahead of its time.

Throughout all this expansion and expense, Jameson and Son had remained very much a family concern. Eventually it became a private limited company in 1891 and a public company 11 years later. During this time the size of the distillery grew and grew and its remains, of castle-like proportions, can still be found between Bow Street and Smithfield, its entrances now bricked up, where once the massive arches had fronted narrow cobbled streets and lanes.

The cellars which ran warren-like below Dublin's streets were long-famed for their holding of Jameson's prized whiskeys. The company had been slow to bottle under their own name, instead preferring to sell their make to merchants who bottled it themselves under a wide variety of titles. But even so, never did its reputation ever diminish. Along with Powers, it was considered the finest Irish pot still whiskey money could buy.

But in 1966 came the famous merger and five years later the long tradition of whiskey production at Bow Street Distillery, spanning perhaps some 200 years, came to an end. For a while Jameson was produced just across the Liffey by Power until that, too, closed and Midleton, in Ireland's deep south, became its new and unlikely home.

When Barnard began his tour of Ireland, his first stop was Bow Street. But it is a strange fact that before he arrived he made the small detour to St Michan's Church where, in the legendary crypt, he gazed upon the mummified remains of several bodies including a nun and a crusader, with their features, skin and nails, still intact. Just yards away stood the busiest distillery in the world, a picture of Victorian vitality, hope and grandeur. When I retraced Barnard's steps in researching this book I touched the same leathered hands when I found those mummies in an almost identical state of suspended decay as he had. Outside it was a quite different matter, however. The distillery buildings, bar those now turned into offices and a museum, were barely intact and had suffered horribly since the distillery's closure only 20 years ago. Their magnificently classic proportions are still there to admire, but for how much longer? Yet while the mummies remained entombed, silent and soulless, at least the spirit of Jameson lives on, albeit 125 miles away.

Jameson Brand History

It is hard to believe that the world's top selling Irish whiskey was not introduced onto the market in bottled form until as recently as 1968. For centuries Jameson sold their whiskey by the cask and individual bonding companies then sold Jameson under their own labels around the world.

Jameson did hit back by initially introducing Crested Ten, but it was the introduction of Red Seal, to a design similar to the present Jameson bottling, which lit the touch paper for success. Although Jameson always came second to Power's in popularity on the home Irish market, it achieved abroad much greater acclaim. So when Pernod-Ricard took over Irish Distillers in 1988, they made the commercial decision to plough all their marketing resources behind two whiskeys: Jameson's and Bushmills.

The result is that Jameson's accounts for nearly 75% of all Irish whiskey sold. Apart from its high marketing profile, its success can also be put down to some judicious blending: it has been specifically designed to appeal to as wide a cross-section of people as possible.

Its pot still/grain content is about 50/50, although a trademark softness suggests the grain has the greater say and a large number of fresh ex-bourbon casks are used which would help dampen down some of the pot still's higher notes. For years I had been told that even some malt from Bushmills went into this blend but I have recently been corrected that this has never been the case. Sherry casked whiskey is used here as well, perhaps to around the 10% mark.

Tasting Notes

Nose	There is a pot still mustiness which is very reminiscent of the original Jameson distillery, but no particular note takes command. Amid the soft murkiness a lemon-drop sharpness gives the nose a playful tweak and as you acclimatise, a certain sherry sweetness is evident as well.
Taste	A sweet start in the mouth bodes well, and as this fades away sooner than expected the mouth feel takes over, being very soft and luxurious for the first few seconds. The middle is a basic mixture of malt and vanillas.
Finish	Dry all along the line with a quite powerful grain dominance; towards the end some pot still crispness comes into play.
Comment	The pot still character has perhaps become more pronounced over the last couple of years, but this still remains a very easy-going, inoffensive whiskey which has been designed, with enormous success, to ap-

peal to a broad spectrum of spirit drinkers — that is why it is one of the fastest-growing spirit brands in the world. Pleasant, enjoyable quaffing.

JAMESON CRESTED TEN

JOHN JAMESON & SON

CRESTED TEN
WHISKEY

by John Jameson & Son, Dublin.
Distillers of Fine Whiskey since 1780.

John Jameson & Son
Bow Street, Dublin 7

BOW STREET DISTILLERY DUBLIN
PRODUCT OF IRELAND

40% vol.   700 ml ℮

Brand History

The Irish are a lucky people. I can count the number of times I've seen this whiskey in pubs in England, Scotland and Wales on both hands. In Ireland, though, and the Republic in particular, it is found in a great many pub as and bars and is regarded as something that little bit special — which it certainly is.

Sadly, it appears to be only older men, those in their 40s and upwards, who drink it. This is odd when you consider that this has an all-round appeal to suit anyone who enjoys a rich pot still character with some quite confident sherry. There is even a slight sweetness which might appeal to the ladies.

Perhaps it's a matter of perception: Crested Ten is Jameson's oldest bottled brand in Ireland. It was launched in 1963 to meet Power's Gold Label and Paddy head on and it was that generation which first learned about its most delightful charms. Although other drinkers have followed suit it is the standard

Jameson brand which has taken seniority status by way of sales.

Crested Ten is more expensive than standard Jameson's. The whiskeys used in it begin at eight years old and the above-average sherry-cask pot still is aged anything between 10 and 15 years. Also there is more pot still than grain. This is a whiskey which traditionally sells well in the winter but is sufficiently light in character and generally too good to be ignored in the summer.

Tasting Notes

Nose   An impressive sherry start is well-matched by pot still sharpness, spice and a hint of melon and ginger. Deliciously Irish.

Taste   Sits in the mouth wonderfully, kicking off with an extremely soft sherry-maltiness and then becomes quite warm and spicy. Throughout there is a delightful sweetness which is perfectly counterbalanced by a rumbling buzz of spice and some brooding bourbon-chocolate notes.

Finish   Extremely classy. The grain does start making an impact here but this is high quality stuff and seemingly well-aged and mild-mannered. The sherry also comes back for a short encore.

Comment   This is a whiskey of great finesse which is balanced beautifully between sweet and dry, light notes and heavy ones. Like all great Irish whiskeys, for the most satisfying results, this should not be sipped but taken by the mouthful and swallowed slowly.

JAMESON 1780

Brand History

In the mid 1980s Jameson had a problem. For years they had been selling a 12-year-old which had been distilled at their old Bow Street Distillery. It was quite a heavy whiskey with some sherry character. But Bow Street had been closed for some time and stocks were becoming dangerously low. A replacement whiskey had to be found. Jameson also produced an even heavier 15-year-old which was in a similarly precarious position. So Jameson decided to scrap both whiskeys and produce a 12-year-old which would stand out as their premier brand.

Today Jameson 1780 remains just that. It has a pot still/sherry infusion like no other whiskey on earth and of all their current blends has the closest characteristics to the old Bow Street distillate.

At least a third of the casks used in this brand are ex-sherry and pot still whiskey accounts for 75% of the blend. Boasting an age statement of 12 years, the average age of the whiskeys used is way above that with healthy amounts of older whiskeys included, some of them going back to 1976 distillations.

This started life as a whiskey designed for the Irish market and today is still found all too rarely abroad, although I have spotted it around some duty-frees.

Tasting Notes

Nose Lush and confident, spicy and warming, there is a prevailing oloroso undercurrent from which it is very hard to pull away.

Taste This is a whiskey which fills the mouth, first with sweet sherry, then the unmistakable delights of old pot still coupled with a short but effective flypast of spice. In fact the pot still dominates, quite a trick when the sherry is so evident. Extremely full-bodied and hard to spot the grain.

Finish Medium length to long. The pot still hangs around, but as it loosens its grip the sherry comes back on song; then that, too, fades and the grain finally gets in to make a dry, vanilla-intense contribution.

Comment It is all too easy to overdo the sherry but this is a whiskey of great charm and poise which has got everything in proportion. I rate Irish Distiller's blender Barry Walsh one of the best in the world. When he told me he regards this whiskey as his favourite I was not surprised. Much hard work and skill has gone into getting this one right. Excellent.

JAMESON DISTILLERY RESERVE

AGED **12** YEARS

JAMESON

DISTILLERY RESERVE

IRISH WHISKEY

Matured in
Oak Casks for not less than
twelve years

40%vol.   PRODUCT OF IRELAND   700ml ℮

DISTILLED, MATURED AND SPECIALLY BOTTLED BY JOHN JAMESON & SON, BOW ST, DUBLIN 7

Brand History

It is not often you will see this whiskey on someone's sideboard or in a bar. If you do, they have either been to the Midleton Distillery or been the beneficiary of someone who has. This is probably the most exclusive of all Ireland's whiskeys. It was created in 1992 to mark the opening of the Jameson Heritage Centre at Midleton Distillery. The style is very close to the Jameson 1780, though for my money not so well-balanced.

But if anyone is a great fan of heavily sherried whiskey, then this is the ultimate experience as far as Ireland is concerned. The make-up is similar to 1780 with over a third of all the whiskey used having been matured in ex-sherry casks and around 75% of the blend being pot still. My guess is that the sherry casks they use are the fullest bodied oloroso they can find, hence the sweetness and intensity. Certainly the pot still plays a less important role than in the 1780.

As it can be bought only at the distillery, sales are relatively low and this helps explain why such sherry-rich casks have been selected. They don't have to vat this one very often so they can be more selective. A must for any serious whiskey drinker.

| **Tasting Notes** |

Nose   Another intense sherry start with the sweet wine being a little more heavy-handed than in the 1780. Despite the sherry dominance, the Irish pot still comes through loud and clear. A little grain also makes its presence felt, as do warming peppers.

Taste   It begins honey-sweet and rich, though not overly complex. Apart from the sherry and pot still, few other notes come through at first, but this is a brooding whiskey, heavy and intense.

Finish   Some grain returns but there is an unusual saltiness about. It dries quite dramatically and where many Irish whiskeys are let down by their finish, this certainly isn't. It is the most complex part of the malt, refusing to die with sweet and sour waves lapping against the tastebuds until the tide, after what seems an age, decides to go out. Wonderful stuff.

Comment   This is the Macallan of the Irish whiskey world. Easily the most sherry-dominant of all the country's whiskeys. Oddly the middle, although no slouch, is the most disappointing, but the finish is something else. If you visit the distillery and don't buy yourself a bottle, you are doing yourself a serious disservice.

BOW STREET

Tasting Notes

From Wm Cadenhead. Distilled 1963, bottled 1991 68.1% abv

Nose   Warming mixture of spice and citrus, some hint of bourbon but pot still remains healthy here. Some orange peel and toffee. Sweet and well-structured.

Taste   Very sweet start, heaps of toffee, fudge and malt and a minty coolness. The middle is firm and beautifully rounded.

Finish   Massive malt and very sweet. Hangs around for a long time refusing to budge.

Comment   This is a stupendous whiskey of the very highest order. By no means complex, but it doesn't have to be. Some old Irish pot still has managed to stay the course but it is the sweet cleanness of this whiskey which allows it to stand so tall. No off-notes at all, really. The cask must have been of the top order, and so too was the whiskey. A classic.

Kilbeggan

Distillery History

It is impossible not to visit John Locke's Kilbeggan Distillery and fail to be moved. It is as if the making of Irish whiskey from a century or more ago has been held in a time warp. Kilbeggan may be the Gaelic for 'little church', but it is a cathedral among the world's distilleries. As it sits proud and splendid beside the River Brusna, it is a picture of charm and tranquillity, but once it was a place of intrigue and dubious practice. Although there was never a bad word said against the whiskey it made, those who ran the distillery were much maligned and in the 1950s when money was tight and the distillery needed all the help it could get, it fell by the wayside, tarnished by unproven accusation.

How a distillery is founded and builds up a great name is usually a fascinating tale often involving people of extraordinary insight and energy. Kilbeggan is no different, but as distilleries go, it is the events of its later years which particularly catch the imagination.

It began life in 1757 as a more modest concern than the fine old building that can be seen today. It is thought the man behind it was Gustavus Lambert, the most important landowner in the immediate district. As the first distillery was built, materials from an old Cistercian monastery on the site were used to aid construction.

John Locke's involvement in the distillery dates from the mid 19th-century and it was he who built it into a business of major importance in the Irish whiskey trade. Its highs and lows, though, reflected the turbulence of the Irish whiskey market with the fortunes of the company peaking, like so many other distillers, between the 1860s and the turn of the century.

The 1920s and 30s were make or break years for Ireland's distillers. Most of them broke. Somehow Locke's clung on, even though their trading, like their management, was weak. They survived only by the strength of their good name, but there was limited demand for Irish pot still whiskey and what demand there was appeared to be satisfied by Powers and Jamesons.

The passing of the Second World War and Locke's fortunate situation as an operational company should have put it in a strong position to flourish since there was a serious worldwide shortage of whiskey. But the company found itself without sufficent stocks to capitalise on this rare opening. One reason, Andrew Bielenberg claims in his history of the distillery, was because much of the whiskey it produced was being siphoned off for the black market. The alleged scam was being worked by middle-management with the aid of the revenue officer. While they grew rich, the company was being bled dry.

If that was the case, then the capping irony was that while it went on undetected for years, the name of the distillery finally fell into disrepute after being implicated in a scandal of which it was entirely innocent. In 1947 the distillery had at last been put up for sale as a going concern. The best offer came from a Swiss syndicate, but what initially looked like a straightforward business transaction turned firstly into a farce, then a whodunnit and finally a matter of rancour and uproar within the Irish Government. When a £75,000 deposit was not forthcoming from the Swiss, the solicitor and auctioneer dealing with the sale began to smell a rat. They alerted both police and officials from the Department of Justice.

When the syndicate's interpreter was found, it was discovered he was travelling on a forged English passport. He had given his name as Horace Smith, but in fact he was Alexander Maximoe and wanted by the British police. On his deportation to Britain he managed to disappear on the Holyhead ferry and at first was thought dead. It transpired, however, that he had been picked up by another boat in which he had arranged to make his escape.

Since the auctioneer involved in the mystery was a Fianna Fail senator, his political enemies tried to make capital out of the strange goings on. A tribunal was set up to look into why the Irish Government appeared happy to sell one of Ireland's most famous names to foreigners of questionable integrity. The findings were that the syndicate's sole aim was to sell the stocks of 60,000 gallons of whiskey on the British black market. Although the Government was cleared of any improper dealings, the mud stuck and the Fianna Fáil party, which was already having a rough time of it, lost even more support.

It was also the end of the road for the distillery. It limped on until 1953 when the stills were shut down for the last time. Some of the whiskey stocks were sold off, but some remained at the distillery and this was finally sold with the buildings to a Karl Heinz Mellow for a mere £10,000 in 1963. He marketed this ageing pot still as Old Galleon, a few cases of which were sold in Ireland, with the majority being off-loaded in Germany.

Meanwhile the famous old distillery was turned, quite literally, into a pigsty. Porkers were in the converted buildings for many years while the distilling apparatus was left largely untouched. That was until the early 70s when the four pot stills were sold off to a scrap dealer. Just a week later the copper market failed. If only copper prices had dropped a week before the sale, these marvellous artefacts might still be in existence.

By the 1980s the possibilities of turning the distillery into a museum — and with it bringing tourists into the Irish midlands — were plainly clear. The Kilbeggan Development Association rented the distillery from its new owner, Powerscreen, and began a programme of renovation. In 1987 Cooley Distillery bought the entire site from the directors of Powerscreen and since then the old Kilbeggan Distillery has again been part of the whiskey industry. Work began immediately on turning the warehouses back to a fit state to house Cooley's forthcoming distillate and by the early 1990s the deafening hammering of coopers repairing damaged casks could once again be heard reverberating around the ancient buildings. Meanwhile Cooley had agreed to lease other sections of the building, mainly those holding the old mash tun and fermenters, back to the KDA for a peppercorn rent of £1 a year for the next 99 years in order to guarantee the distillery as a vital site of industrial archaeology.

The redundant old pot stills from Tullamore were

then brought by Cooley to Kilbeggan and it was hoped that perhaps one day distilling could begin again at John Locke's old distillery. Detailed plans have been drawn up to make a traditional pot still whiskey but it would cost £1.5 million. There are now cheaper plans afoot to mash and ferment the pot still at Cooley and bring the wash to Kilbeggan to distil in the old Tullamore stills. That operation would be a fraction of the cost.

But with Cooley having problems enough keeping their own plant operational it seems very unlikely. But wouldn't life be a dull thing without the occasional romantic dreams of the optimist and visionary? After all, wasn't that how most distilleries began in Ireland?

THE OLD TULLAMORE STILLS LIE FORLORNLY OUTSIDE KILBEGGAN DISTILLERY

John Locke's and Kilbeggan

Brand Histories

The future is always more important than the past as far as spirit brands are concerned and there are no more vital examples of this in Irish whiskey than Locke's and Kilbeggan.

Once, they were two famous names slugging it out in a shrinking market. Today, after a long period of obsolescence, they are exactly the opposite and represent an extraordinary breakthrough in the ending of the monopolistic control of Irish whiskey. Tyrconnell single malt was the first out of the Cooley stable once their oldest grain stocks had matured to the three years minimum required by law.

The actual arrival of Kilbeggan and Locke's on the market was delayed by Irish Distillers' unsuccessful attempt to buy out Cooley Distillery and smother the brands at birth. Monopoly regulations have for the meantime prevented IDG's moves, but Cooley must now perform in overseas markets in a way that IDG have so far failed to do if they are to remain independent and a cash influx must be forthcoming if Cooley is to survive. Aside from these considerations things have started well. Over the next year Kilbeggan will be found in the Netherlands, Switzerland, Northern Ireland, USA, France, Germany and in the UK Locke's should soon be making an entry.

Older Irish drinkers will remember both these brands as pure pot still. They are now both blends with Locke's being a slightly heavier version of Kilbeggan. The brands were sculpted by independent blender Jimmy Lang, once of Chivas and creator of the famous Passport Scotch brand, with the aid of Noel Sweeney of Cooley Distillery. For these blends Jimmy used some of the slightly later malts which had improved greatly from the first run. Considering he had only a single malt and single grain to work with, it was a pretty impressive first go.

As the malt and grain matures, the blends look set to get better and better, a fairly lip-smacking prospect.

Locke's Tasting Notes

Nose   Some sweet, malty notes, but rather hard to find amid a coarse astringency.

Taste   Sweet and smooth at first, becoming much fuller bodied and slightly anarchic. It has a wonderful middle of malt and spice and an irrepressible honeyed sweetness which works busily around the palate, filling the mouth. At times it runs over the taste-buds like the smoothest of engines, then splutters about a bit. But, impressively, at no time does it lose its balance.

Finish   The powerful maltiness trails off leaving the grain which is first noticeable as the conveyor of ex-bourbon cask vanillins and then as a slight off-key bitterness.

Comment Ignore the nose, which isn't all that great. This was a blend designed to be drunk and a very enjoyable one it is, too. Perfect fun for any time of day or night.

Kilbeggan Tasting Notes

Nose Very similar to Locke's; a touch sweeter and heavier perhaps, with a certain orange and spice effect. Better balanced.

Taste A very soft start heralds a quite complex bitter-sweet blend where the malt dominates the grain for the early and middle stages.

Finish Continues in this same gentle vein yet never relents in its full-flavoured malty at-

tack. Like Locke's the grains do enter into the fray late on and bring with them a bitterness derived from the wood.

Comment   Quite similar in every way to Locke's except that the middle is far more forceful and the nose has some charm. The dying rays of the finish are not quite so accomplished, though.

MIDLETON

Distillery History

The town of Midleton, located a mile or two inland
from the south coast and equidistant between Cork
and Youghal, hence its name, is one like any other in
Ireland. It has a main thoroughfare in which all the
shops can be found and the pavements, as seems
peculiar to Ireland, are constantly busy by day with
people going about their daily business, and by night
are crowded with people as the many pubs are visited and revisited.

The buildings are well-constructed and pleasing
to the eye, especially when the sun illuminates them,
but are by no means outstanding. Tucked away,
though, behind the shops on the east side of the main
street lies not one, but two distilleries. The one that
can be seen through the gates as you cross the old
bridge which has taken you into Midleton from the
Cork road has a splendour about it which momentar-
ily halts you in your tracks. But on entering the building, you would fear that this is just another Kilbeggan:
ancient, proud but obsolete.

But whereas virtually every other whiskey-making
town in Ireland has at one time or another, over the
last 200 years, failed, Midleton somehow has succeeded. It still makes whiskey. But not in the 18th-
century buildings which boast its original stills, because a few hundred yards beyond some trees sits
the distillery which now accounts for the spirit which
matures to make up the whiskey for all the Jameson

brands — Paddy, Power's, Midleton Rare, Hewitts, Dunphys, Redbreast, Green Spot, and Tullamore Dew.

Unique to any distillery in the world, the stills are not only the last to make pure Irish pot still, a mixture of malted and unmalted barley, but when required they also produce a pure single malt and, in the patent stills, varying types of grain whiskey to suit individual blends.

Why Midleton should have survived is really a matter of good fortune and fate. It has always been known for making good pot still, but no better than some distilleries which were well-known to drinkers four or five generations ago, or long-forgotten names now found as brands that are much lighter blends. To the purist, it must seem unjust and ironic that these distilleries, purpose-built by men of vision and often at great personal hardship, should today be lost or at best lie in varying states of rack and ruin, while Midleton may have never become a distillery at all had not Marcus Lynch's textile business failed. But let us be thankful it ever made whiskey at all.

It was Lynch who, for the then massive outlay of £20,000, erected the sturdy buildings of Midleton after leasing the site from Viscount Midleton on May 20th, 1796. The woollen manufacturing business had been operating for only a short while before the British army, expanding their forces to meet the threat of Napoleon, bought the land and the mill which they converted into barracks for soldiers and stabling for their horses.

Lynch was later able to lease back the buildings but by the 1820s the mill was lying empty, free from both the captains of industry and of warfare. The Government sold the property to the Archbishop of Cashel and on his death his brother, Lord Midleton, was again able to acquire the land. He had not had it long before he sold it to three brothers, James, Daniel and Jeremiah Murphy on December 20th, 1825. It was they who knew exactly the purpose the fine buildings should be turned to: the making of whiskey.

One of the most astonishing features of the distillery is a cast iron water-wheel built in 1852 to replace the old wooden one. It was the Murphys who secured the use of the waterway needed to turn it and power the raking equipment inside the mash tuns.

When Daniel retired from the firm, the distillers called themselves James Murphy & Co. It was continued as a strictly family concern, although some members left the distilling side to set up the Murphy Brewery in Cork. But although they were a close-knit family, they were very astute business partners and it was James Murphy who hit upon consolidating the company by merging it with the distilleries operating in Cork.

The Cork distillers of North Mall, The Watercourse, The Green and Daly's all saw the economic wisdom behind the move and the possibility of closing operating plants, shedding jobs and thus saving money. In those days distilling was labour intensive, employing anything between 150 and 300 people at every distillery. After a series of meetings they finalised their plans and on the December 23rd, 1867, just days after Murphy's 42nd anniversary, the Cork Distilleries Company was formed, with Murphy's officially being sold into the group the following year.

James Murphy was appointed the CDC's first managing director and the company thrived. Distilling was confined to just the two plants, Midleton and North Mall which continued to make its then world-famous Wise's Cork Old Pot-Still Whisky. Watercourse ceased distilling but carried on malting and warehousing, and the making of whiskey also stopped at both the Green Distillery and Daly's which were used for warehousing and as granaries.

That Midleton should have continued distilling is not really that surprising. Situated in the countryside it was not subject to city overheads and perhaps more importantly, the wash still holding 31,648 gallons was the largest pot still in the world. The distillery, with a Coffey still on site, had access as well to the making of blended whiskey if so desired. For over 100 years nothing really changed at Midleton. The Coffey still was replaced, as late as 1962, by a German-made continuous still, but that was the extent of the changes made.

The whiskey continued to be made in their giant wash still and even the men responsible for its quality were all members of one family. In the 1880s it was a Mr A. Ross, whose own father had managed Midleton, who escorted Barnard around the distillery and it was Sandy Ross, whose father had also been manager, who was the site superintendent of the distillery nearly a century later as it entered its final days.

Ireland is well-known for its tall tales and miracles. None, though, are more astonishing than the one regarding Sandy, who was fortunate in the extreme to still be around to follow in his father and grandfather's footsteps. He had been working in the still room standing beside a pot still when the copper exploded and he was blown clean out of the building through a window. Just moments before, he had been going about his daily business, but seconds later found himself on the cold gravel outside, surrounded by a cluster of startled and amused workmates. Worse still, he was totally naked save for a shirt collar that gripped limpet like to his neck and the belt of his trousers which hung limply around his waist. Apart from a few scratches and his bruised dignity, he was otherwise in one piece. The management, in a radical fit of touching kindness, gave him the rest of the day off — provided he turned up for work at the usual time next morning!

The old Midleton distillery would probably have continued in its present form had Cork Distilleries Co, in 1966, not decided to join forces with their Dublin opposition John Jameson and John Power to form the Irish Distillers Group. The new company agreed that an all-purpose pot and column still needed to be built and Midleton had the space for this development on available and cheaper ground, whereas the Dublin distilleries, hemmed in close to the city centre, had little or no room in which to expand. They could also raise cash by selling off some of the city property.

As the new plant took shape the making of whiskey continued as usual at Midleton as if nothing was happening. One evening in July 1975 the men clocked off as usual from the old distillery. The following morning they returned, but instead of entering the old, historic buildings, they walked on an extra few hundred yards and began producing the first make from the new stills.

Their environment couldn't have been much more different. Their old place of work had been an 18th-century building steeped in tradition where the smell of grist and spirit was as much a part of the structure as the bricks and mortar. Now they were entering a distillery from a different age. From the outside it could have been a factory which made dogfood or processed plastics. There was no sense of tradition, no looking back at the past. It was designed for the specific purpose of making the stuff which would bring high quality Irish whiskey back to the forefront of the world spirit market as efficiently as possible.

There were no goodbyes from the men for the old plant; no closing or opening ceremonies; it was just part of a day's work. However, for the Head Distiller, Barry Crockett, it had to be a wrench. He was actually born in one of the Georgian buildings within the original distillery.

Although the tools with which they were making the whiskey were markedly different, the way it was made stayed the same. The stillhouse was, and still is, a truly extraordinary sight to behold. The stillhouse at the old building was cramped and divided into two sections with the giant wash still awarded more or less a room of its own. At the new Midleton the pot stills, sharing the same great hall as the grain stills, were not the traditional bulbous affairs like their predecessors and also those once found at Power, Tullamore, Royal Irish and the like. These stills were of the squatter swan-necked style preferred in Scotland and at Bushmills. They also are smaller than old Irish pot stills, yet bigger than anything in Scotland. As you stand beside them, dwarfed by their bulk and height, you are reminded more of grazing brontosaurs rather than graceful swans.

Another feature are the wash backs. Once made of wood, at the new complex they are stainless steel affairs built in such a manner that they actually form the outer walls of the buildings. This is curious, because the wash is then subject to a variance in outside temperatures, which theoretically could affect the brewing process; but it is all part of the Midleton idiosyncratic distilling style.

But what of the other distilleries that made up the

Cork Distilleries Company? Since 1920 Midleton has been distilling pot still whiskey alone. In that year the North Mall Distillery was wrecked by fire and never distilled again. It was a sad loss: the distillery was one of Ireland's oldest, built in 1779 on a island, once the home of an old Dominican Friary. But some of the buildings did survive the inferno, and in one of them some of their smaller brands of whiskeys, like Midleton Very Rare and Hewitts, are today blended. Indeed, one of the vats in which the blending is carried out is over 100 years old, dating back to when North Mall was one of the most impressive sites in the glorious city of Cork. As well as the blending operation, there is also a bottling plant, installed in 1964.

Another of the buildings which survives is the house once lived in by the owners of the distillery, the Wise family. The family died out with bachelor Francis Wise, a noted miser, who built false walls onto the outside of the property to give visitors the appearance that he lived in a grander house than he actually did.

Elsewhere in Cork are the remains of the Watercourse Distillery (see Hewitts), and although The Green Distillery was reopened to make gin and Vodka for the company until the 1970s, with the advent of Midleton, whose column stills now carry out that task, The Green and John Street are now gone, leaving only the old distillery at Midleton for Irish whiskey lovers to gaze upon and admire.

Brand History

It is rare to chart the full evolution of an Irish whiskey, but with Midleton Very Rare it is possible. In hotels and pubs throughout Ireland the odd bottle of Midleton VR can be found either on the whiskey shelf or languishing deep in the cellar. If you do come across bottlings of VR, you may be able to sample each vintage over a period of time.

When it was launched in 1984 it contained not only the whiskeys which have developed from Midleton's opening in 1975, but to give some extra depth, a few casks from the old Midleton Distillery. For blender Barry Walsh, working on Midleton Very Rare has been a learning curve. As each year passed he discovered more and more about what the whiskey was capable of achieving during maturation. This fact is reflected in the styles of the whiskeys bottled between 1984 and now. The earlier bottlings did not hang together too well with the grain not really gelling with the pot still. On reflection it seems a pity the Midleton used from the original distillery was not bottled on its own. Still, the intention was honourable.

However, over the years there have been noticeable changes. There is obviously less grain now in comparison to the brand's infancy and instead of putting together casks which appeared to fit the bill, special casks are now put to one side exclusively to make up Midleton VR. These casks are called 'B1s', which are bourbon casks fresh from the USA. The whiskeys now used range from 12-year-olds to 1976s and the Midleton VR of today is a very fine drink indeed.

It remains highly exclusive and rather expensive. Only between 600 and 1200 cases are sold each year and it enjoys a worldwide market. And the good news is that after the disappointing start, it just seems to be getting better and better.

Midleton VR 1984 Tasting Notes

Nose Velvety soft and nothing like the pot still character one might have expected. There is malt, but it is Highland in style, leaving the grain to steal the show. Some nutmeg essence does give a little character.

Taste Very sweet, very soft and very grainy. Hardly any middle or backbone to this at all.

Finish Bitter off-notes cling to the palate and fade reluctantly. Some malt and toffee lurking, but this doesn't get a look-in against such a strong grain imbalance.

Comment Disappointing to say the least. No balance here and the metallic finish ruins it completely.

Midleton VR 1985 Tasting Notes

Nose   A nudge on from the '84 vintage thanks to a better defined malt presence and a tell-tale harshness of unmalted barley. Still sweet but some oiliness in there, too. A gentle bourbon character is quite fruity and there are some roasted nuts lurking about also. Much more complex than its predecessor.

Taste   A pretty decent start: medium-bodied and oily with a nutty maltiness. The middle is still a little thin, though.

Finish   This starts well enough with a spiciness which wasn't around for the '84. But again the grain is rather bitter and overpowering at the very end. Not as forbidding as the previous vintage, but still far too hostile.

Comment A great improvement on the first attempt. Much better balanced but the finish is still letting the side down a little.

Midleton VR 1986 Tasting Notes

Nose   Now starting to become quite heavy with an emphatic pot still/fruit character which takes over, whereas the ex-bourbon had previously held sway. If I didn't have it from the horse's mouth that this didn't have any sherry, I would swear it had.

Taste   Sweet start and immediately spicy. The pot still maltiness takes much longer to make its mark. Very rich, indeed.

Finish   The malt now comes into its own, but halfway through this rather long finale the grain makes it's first noticeable appearance which just brings the quality down a peg or two.

Comment An altogether richer whiskey than in previous years. At last it is beginning to form a character of its own and is becoming quite impressive.

96

Midleton VR 1987 Tasting Notes

Nose   The closest thing to consistency yet. Very much like the '86 but with a tell-tale mustiness making this not quite as well-balanced.

Taste   Again sweet, but the sweetness doesn't linger quite so long and the spiciness nips in very quickly indeed. There is a change: a trace of menthol, or something equally cooling appears on the palate.

Finish   Some woody notes muscle in quite quickly here to give a lopsided thinness with none of the lush character of the previous year. However, like cavalry charging to the rescue, some very powerful pot still comes through at the finish to give some last minute, high quality relief to this vintage.

Comment   Quite a complex whiskey, not overly satisfying in some places, but delightful in others. The injury-time pot still is a cracker, though.

Midleton VR 1988 Tasting Notes

Nose   The character now has been pulled away from a fruity influence. The pot still is the sharpest yet. Rather uncluttered, striking and simple. Oh, and a touch of honey and mint make a surprising but very low-key entrance.

Taste   The very sweet start of old is gone; a shrill pot still hardness whistles about the tastebuds followed by a bourbon-cask induced spiciness. It's so busy that at no time does it settle to allow a recognisable middle to be formed.

Finish   Still sweet now and the pot still maltiness battles it out with some grain which is in pretty good nick. A dryness arrives, but takes its time about it.

Comment   A tangible link here between the 1988 and

1993. Showing the very first signs of becoming the Midleton Very Rare we know today.

Midleton VR 1989 Tasting Notes

Nose Citrousy and spicy, the malt is hard chiselled into the overall character. The pot still is quite formidable, as well.

Taste The best start yet. It begins like pure pot still; very vivid in the mouth and filling every last crevice. But for the first time in a few years the grain makes an early entrance. Having said that, they sit by each other well.

Finish Very hard and brittle, the unmalted barley is particularly noticeable here: you feel you could almost crunch your teeth on it. Quite extraordinary.

Comment In some ways I think this is the best yet, but it still does not have quite the balance which the latter-day vintages exude with their wonderful spiciness.

Midleton VR 1990 Tasting Notes

Nose Carrying on where the '89 left off. Perhaps the hard pot still does not drill itself quite so far into your sinuses: this is more of a masseuse, gently caressing the senses.

Taste Solid pot still again. There is a pattern now: pot still first, sweeter maltier notes second, pleasant grains third and somewhere, imperceptibly, warming spices fill in the gaps.

Finish Very long and almost like a Redbreast in its pot still intensity. The bourbon wood used does add that now familiar spiciness for the very first time. Truly astounding whiskey: if you come across it, you must sample it.

Midleton VR 1991 Tasting Notes

Nose   Much softer and far less ebullient than the last couple of vintages. Malty but with limited complexity. Not quite boring, but not far from it, either.

Taste   Makes amends on the palate, but again we are back to sweetness first then low-key pot still flavour following. In its favour it is a honeyed sweetness and the overall feel is beautifully lush.

Finish   Disappointing compared to previous years. The lack of pot still dominance means that the grain has a larger say than it ought. In this case it's not particularly interesting.

Comment   The one blip over recent years. More like an '87 or '85 than one of the brave new pot still vintages which has made this such an outstanding Irish whiskey. Worth tasting in an hotel, but don't bother with a bottle.

Midleton VR 1992 Tasting Notes

Nose   Different to anything that's gone before. A spiciness dominates for the first time. Oddly, not a million miles off the 1985, but cleaner and with more pot still. And cloves?

Taste   Very rich and magnificently full-bodied. A very oily beginning and middle and clinging to it is a significant pot still deliciousness mixed with just the right amount of warming, tingling spice with a rich, sweet counterbalance.

Finish   Very long, intense malt and hardly any trace of grain until the very last notes come through and hit the back of the roof of the mouth with a metallic thud. Superb, nonetheless.

Comment   This is a real fun whiskey last thing at night. You can take a glass and spend quite some time trying to work out what it's going to do next.

Midleton VR 1993 Tasting Notes

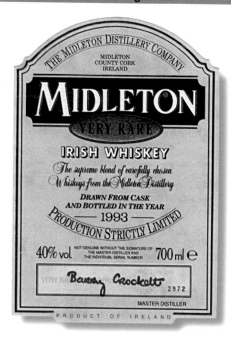

Nose	Some real pot still character bubbles proudly through. There is also an impressive sub-strata of honey and pepper and some very faint and inexplicable sherry-type fruitiness.
Taste	Dry start, the harshness of the pot still grabs the tastebuds and dominates. The malt is also very strong and holds together the pot still/bourbon cask middle. A real lip-smacker.

Finish   Very long and malty with some spiciness but it is the very high quality, malty Irish pot still which wins the day.

Comment   This is the tenth bottling of Midleton Very Rare and is scarcely recognisable from the highly disappointing whisky which began it all in 1984. Now there is real pot still character and it noses and tastes like a whiskey made at Midleton. It is better than the '92: it's less spicy, perhaps, but the overall complexity is quite beguiling. It's big, brash and beautiful.

PADDY

Brand History

There is something about the way Paddy whisky was so named that you can't help feeling it could only happen in Ireland. During the 1920s and 30s there were two whiskeys which could be easily bought by the bottle. The first and most popular was Power's Gold Label. The second was CDC's Old Irish Whiskey, which, as good as it might have been when it slipped down the throat, was not the easiest brand name to trip off the tongue.

In the counties which made up the south-west region, collectively called Munster, Cork Distilleries had a sales rep of some repute, Paddy Flaherty. He would breeze into town on his bike, and as he did so men would scamper into the bar to be there to greet him. It was a well-known fact that if you were in close proximity as he ordered his glass, this most generous and gregarious of fellows would stand you a round.

It was his way of making sure everyone got a taste for the whiskey and put pressure on the publicans to always have some in stock. If they were running low or, heaven forbid, had actually run out, they immediately contacted the distillery asking for another case of 'Paddy Flaherty's whiskey'.

It did not take long for Cork Distilleries to realise they were on to a winner here. Firstly, they put the name Paddy Flaherty at the foot of the label to show it was, indeed, the real stuff. Then, by degree, the label altered until they went the whole hog and decided to call it, quite simply, Paddy.

Unfortunately the company did not go as far as to give their number one salesman a bonus or a percentage of the profits they were reaping. By the time he retired from the company he was just another employee.

Of all Ireland's major pot still brands, this was the only one which didn't have to change distilleries when the Irish Distillers Group was formed. But where the whiskey is so markedly different from Paddy Flaherty's day, is that it is now no longer pot still but a blend of pot still and grain, with the blender going easy on the pot still fraction to ensure a very light whiskey.

It is one of the softest of all Ireland's whiskeys. This is because there is relatively little pot still content, but instead the grain works in tandem with single malts from both Midleton and Bushmills to keep any distinctive pot still flavour subdued. At Midleton three different types of pure malt whiskey are produced and Paddy uses the very lightest of them all. Of the three whiskey codes, grain makes up the highest proportion of the blend followed by pot still and then the pure malt, but if you add up the pure malt and pot still, these outweigh the grain content.

Tasting Notes

Nose   Not only is this a grainy nose, it also has an unusual astringent severity for Irish blended whiskey. Best when very well-warmed in the hand. Even then it keeps rather too firm a grip on the pot still. Some sherried fruitiness does come through, though, with a hint of apples, as well.

Taste   Again it's the grain making the first move.

It is quite soft and sweet and mild enough to allow the merest hint of pot still to follow through.

Finish   There is no trace of pot still at all as soon as the middle is passed. The grain starts quite attractively at first, keeping its sweetness in shape. But as it dries, a bitterness descends which hangs about to the very finish.

Comment   This whiskey has merit which is mainly a soft relaxed mood that is crushed by the grain towards the end. But my taste is for pot still character, of which this has very little. If you like your whiskey strong tasting, give this a miss. If you prefer yours light and rather simplistic, then Paddy's yer maun.

JONES ROAD

Distillery History

When, on July 22nd, 1873, the newly-formed Dublin Whiskey Distillery Company (DWC) began its first mash, it was quite a remarkable achievement because it was exactly one year to the day that the building of Dublin's last, and in many ways grandest, distilleries had begun.

Where nearly all of Dublin's other major whiskey distilleries had been started as family concerns, Jones Road was different. It had been built purely as a commercial venture by a group of Dublin businessmen, including a couple of accountants, with no distilling knowledge who employed skilled whiskey men.

The site of the distillery was by far the most breathtaking, and historic, in the city. The site, surrounded by the ruins of a castle and abbey, was on the very spot of the Battlefield of Clontarf, where in 1014, Danish invaders where dealt a mortal blow by King Brian Boru.

To add to the beautiful views from the distillery, (it was even compared by contemporary writers to the Bay of Naples!), the River Tolka flowed through its grounds, although the water for making the whiskey was piped in from the Royal Canal a mile away, thus sharing its water source with John Jameson & Son.

However, as trading became tougher, drastic action was needed at the new distillery. The merger of Powers and Jameson in 1966 was not the first time Dublin distilling giants had forged a partnership. In 1889 DWD merged with two long-established distillers in the city, William Jameson and George Rowe, to form the Dublin Distilling Company. But they continued to produce pure pot still under their own names.

Although between them they had the capacity to produce 3,500,000 gallons of pot still whiskey each year, lack of demand meant they achieved nowhere near that figure. The company limped through the early 20th century, closing one, then another of the distilleries, occasionally reopening them to produce small quantities of new spirit. At last the company gave out and was wound up sometime towards the end of the Second World War.

Tasting Notes

From Wm Cadenhead. Distilled 1942, bottled 1991 65% abv

Nose   Quite wonderful and tremendously rich. A mouth-watering cross between a very powerful, old Kentucky Bourbon or Tennessee whiskey and Christmas pudding. When it has had a little time in the glass a delicious spiciness reminiscent of a freshly opened, but slightly under-ripe, Chateau Margaux or Latour comes through. Extraordinary.

Taste   For a fleeting moment there is smooth pot still, then ... oh dear! There is a burning sensation of the lips and tongue as the mixture of strong alcohol and powerful woody components sear their way into the skin and nerves. The tastebuds take a spicy hammering when their time comes too. A massive malty, peppery attack but totally lacking in grace.

Finish The powerful liquorice feel sits perfectly with the bourbony start and other woody notes hang around, too.

Comment This is one heck of a shock to the system, but in fairness is not an altogether undrinkable whiskey. If it has done this well in the wood it cannot have been anything other than a very fine whiskey when it was originally made. Certainly one to keep rather than drink. But drink it you can.

POWERS

Distillery History

There are few more charming cities to visit than Dublin and an architectural exploration of its winding back streets and substantial main roads offers surprise upon surprise. But none more so for the whiskey lover than when you cross the Liffey by the Father Mathew Bridge, pass by The Brazen Head, Dublin's oldest pub, and turn right into John's Lane. Before your disbelieving eyes is one of the most extraordinary, and to some, saddest sights, in all Ireland.

Exposed to chill winds and lashing rain by winter and basked by the summer's sun, are three pot stills which were, according to Alfred Barnard in 1887 'as bright and keen as burnished gold', but are now faded and a lifeless green. They jut proudly from a brick dais to form a bizarre silhouette against Christchurch Cathedral, which, higher up the hill, looks down upon the sight with a melancholy gothic beauty.

You have just stumbled upon the remains of the demolished stillhouse of the fabled John's Lane Distillery, for nearly two centuries the home of John Power & Son. Fortunately much of the distillery still survives, but today produces artists and sculptors rather than Ireland's most cherished whiskey since it is now the National College of Art and Design.

The famous facade, once known as the Counting House, is unchanged and each detail of illustration in Barnard's book can be accounted for. But not since 1976 has the sweet smell of mashing grist hovered on the winds above the distillery. That was when the final curtain came down on distilling in Dublin — Power had followed in the footsteps of its great rival across the river, Jameson, so that both their whiskeys began to be made from the same brand-new pots and columns at Midleton.

It is unlikely that James Power, a coaching innkeeper of Thomas Street (from where the mails were sent to the north and west of the country), could have foreseen the success of his venture when he founded his tiny distillery in 1791 by converting the hostelry.

His son John had teamed up with him around the turn of the century by which time he had expanded and moved premises just a few hundred yards to John's Lane. Although the business was called James Power & Son in 1804, by 1809 the venture had become a limited company under the name John Power while James remained in charge. Growth was steady until 1823 and then rapid. That happened to be the year when the laws regarding distilling were changed and made life a lot easier for whisk(e)y makers operating legally in both Scotland and Ireland.

In 1823, John Power boasted a 500-gallon still, a fair size for its day, with an annual output of 33,000 gallons — quite an increase from his father's fledgling 6000-gallon output. But ten years later, with the aid of even larger stills, production had increased tenfold and Power's whiskey had arrived in the big time, and has never looked back.

Such success brought wealth and all its glorious trappings and the Power family rose within a generation from innkeepers and speculative distillers to members of Dublin high society. John Power was knighted and later became High Sheriff of Dublin. Such was his standing in the community that it was he who laid the foundation stone for the O'Connell Monument.

Meanwhile the phenomenal growth of the distillery continued. In James Power's time the original distillery was small enough to be powered by horse mill. Within half a century enough money had been accumulated for massive expansion, not just for the materials and apparatus to make ever-increasing amounts of Power's, but also for the storage capacity it required for maturation.

In 1871 the distillery was rebuilt to a classic, Victorian factory style and the lands it occupied covered nearly seven acres stretching from Thomas Street to the Quay. It had become one of the most impressive sights in central Dublin and a vital part of the economy, employing 300 people and bringing cash into the city from a very wide market.

There were two central reasons for Power's impressive empire. The first was the quality of their whiskey. Even Barnard, who gave chapter and verse on every nut and bolt that made a distillery work but was loathe to offer detail or opinion of the whiskey it made, was moved to comment: *'We had previously sampled the firm's make of 1885, which we thought good and most useful, either as a blending or single whisky. The old make, which we drank with our luncheon, was delicious, and finer than anything we had hitherto tasted. It was as perfect in flavour, and as pronounced in the ancient aroma of Irish Whisky so dear to the hearts of connoisseurs, as one could possibly desire, and we found a small flask of it very useful afterwards on our travels.'*

The other was the company's unusually innovative skills. While it turned its back until relatively recently on blending its pot still whisky with grain, it had no such inhibitions with bottling whiskey in any shape or size that would sell. It had been common practice in Ireland for distillers to sell their whiskey by the cask to outlets that would either bottle it or sell direct from the cask. To prevent the possibility of contamination or adulteration, as well as protect their own good name, Power's bottled their own whiskey with a distinctive and now famous gold label. By then one of Ireland's largest distillers, they were nevertheless astute enough to be the first company to sell their whiskey in miniatures called Baby Powers. To achieve that notable first, new government legislation was required. But with the Powers being so formidable a family it was no great surprise that the changes to the law were made.

Such was the distillery's output that by the close of the 19th century Power's ceased floor malting and had begun buying in. Otherwise it remained a traditional pot still distillery until the 1950s when the company finally gave way to trend and installed a continuous still to make grain spirit for blending, a move which would have sent the first John Power and his son spinning in their graves! They had always been opposed to what they had seen as a fouling of their pure Irish whiskey. But in 1932, when Sir Thomas Talbot Power died, there was no one left on the board with the Power name, although it remained within the family through his sisters. The strong family principles continued, but with Irish whiskey struggling —

particularly on the export market — new avenues had to be explored.

The final and most dramatic of outcomes was the merger of the company in 1966 with the other two remaining distilleries in the Irish Republic, Cork Distilleries and their greatest rivals, John Jameson & Son. It was agreed they would move lock, stock and barrel to a new distilling complex at Midleton. And at the same time they also decided to turn their famous all pot still bottled whiskey into one containing a grain distilled at John's Lane.

Typically, it was Power, the oldest distillers in Eire, who were the last to reluctantly quit their post. It was a sad day for Dublin and Irish whiskey in particular. Today, those three massive pot stills defiantly stand their ground, as green as the Irish flag, and as impressive and proud as the whiskey they once made.

Brand History

Just around the corner from the Midleton Distillery where Power's is made today is a very small pub, Mahoney's in Sraid Connail — O'Connell Street. The main window is massive and brightened by a gold and red logo. It reads Power's. It is a sight which jolts the system and draws the whiskey lover inside. On the shelves and optics there are several bottles of Power's whiskey and very little else. When I went in there wasn't a Jameson's in sight.

The elderly owner told me she sold Power's by the crateload. Good news for Irish Distillers — or is it? Once the whiskey for the town was Paddy which was made for decades at Midleton by Cork Distilleries. Then Irish Distillers put their marketing muscle into Jameson's. Yet the drinkers at Mahoney's switched allegiance to Power's. The reason I was given both at the pub and throughout my travels in Ireland was that it was recognised as the best whiskey of the lot. I for one can only enthusiastically agree. To drink at home it is a delight; to drink in an Irish pub counts as one of life's more simple but unforgettable pleasures.

Power's is ridiculously hard to find outside Ireland, even in the UK. Yet it is a whiskey which should always be there somewhere in the cabinet, not only to drink yourself, but also to entertain Irish guests with, for there is no better way of making them feel at home. Power's is still the biggest seller in all-Ireland and has been since they began bottling it in 1894. In those days it was pure pot still whiskey; today Midleton produces a delectable blend of pot still and grain whiskeys with an enormous emphasis on the pot still which, in comparison, makes Jameson appear soft and Paddy almost feeble.

Anyone who has tasted Power's will not be surprised to learn that the make-up of the pot still portion uses 60% unmalted barley to 40% malted barley, the highest ratio of that type produced in Midleton. And, even more significantly, the pot still goes to make up some 70% of the overall blend, quite astonishing when you consider it is priced in the same bracket as Paddy and Jameson! There is no use of single malt whiskey whatsoever and the distillation method used is designed to produce the highest notes possible. This type of whiskey matures well in the cask and reacts perfectly with the wood. The end product is a whiskey which just bursts at the seams with high flavour development.

The whiskey when bottled is known both as Gold Label and Three Swallow. The former is self explanatory, the latter has nothing to do with the birds which flutter around the bottle's neck. It is because it was said you should drink your glass of Power's not in one, but in three swallows. Sound advice, but make sure you keep it in your mouth for a good ten to 15 seconds before it slips down your throat. Then you will see why an entire nation can't be wrong.

Tasting Notes

Nose   The most attractive of all Irish whiskeys. First to show is a massive pot still character which is hard and striking, but this is softened, dissolved almost, by a viscous graininess. The overall effect is a stunning dovetailing of honeyed sweetness and dry, peppery tones. This spice effect comes from the wood which is also present, thanks to the grain, in a creamy vanilla, cream soda gentleness. Glorious stuff.

Taste An immediate explosion of flavours on the palate, most of them spicy. There is a well defined pot still rigidity on which all else hangs, but those honey notes come through strongly and fuse delectably with the spice. The effect is tingling and voluptuous.

Finish Long, sweet and sour with lingering spice. Hangs around in one form or another in different parts of the mouth for several minutes. It's mainly the spice, though, which refuses to die.

Comment This is a monster of a whiskey of which the nose and tastebuds can never tire. Its very best effects can be experienced when drunk at room or pub temperature without ice or water. Once, I preferred Black Bush for all round charm and complexity, but over the last two years I think Power's has improved and familiarity has bred anything but contempt. Classic is an overused cliché in the drinks world, but if this isn't one then I'd like to know what is.

John's Lane

Tasting Notes

From Wm Cadenhead. Distilled 1956. Bottled 1991, 73.2% abv

Nose Very close to pure, unadulterated ancient bourbon. This is of the sweet, flowery variety, a bit like Jim Beam rather than a charcoaled Tennessee.

Taste Erupts immediately on landing with a red hot explosion of not only a distinctive woodiness, but also some surprising sweetness as well. If you can taste beyond the alcohol there is still some maltiness intact, although little sign of delicate pot still.

Finish Surprisingly malty and pleasant. The inferno has abated leaving a quite pleasant malt and liquorice finale, although the wood comes out stronger early on.

Comment Against the odds, drinkable despite the woodiness. That the malt has come through with sweet and dry notes at such an old age, and bearing in mind the cask had been filled without the new make being reduced, is a quite wonderful tribute to those who made Power's all those years ago.

REDBREAST PURE POT STILL

Brand History

Of the many brand names under which Jameson whiskey was found, Redbreast was for a long time one of the better known and most respected. But although it said Redbreast on the label, it acquired the epithet 'The Priest's Bottle' on account that no matter which priest you went to visit, he had a bottle somewhere about the house.

Redbreast was a brand name for Jameson's pure Irish pot still, bottled in bond by Gilbey Vintners of Ireland as a sister whiskey to their Crock of Gold brand. It began life in 1939 with Jameson filling Gilbey's own casks. The make-up of Redbreast was quite simple: for every two ex-sherry casks used, there was an ex-bourbon cask tipped in, too.

The whiskey was sold almost exclusively in Ireland with only a dribble getting into mainland Britain. However, in 1968 Jameson decided to end links with the bonded trade, but Gilbey managed to persuade their suppliers to continue selling them pot still until, in 1971, the Bow Street Distillery was closed.

By the time the last bottling was made in 1985, the whiskey was not quite what it once had been. Many casks aged between 22 and 25 years had to be used, giving the whiskey a tired feel. It can still be seen around bars and hotels and is well worth the couple of pounds for a glass to taste some real history.

The present Redbreast was relaunched by Irish Distillers themselves as their single all pot still whiskey. The heavier style of pot still is used in its vatting with whiskeys of 12 years and upwards being selected. Some sherry casks are used, but the bourbon cask character comes through much more clearly. Still criminally hard to find, inside or outside Ireland, it is beyond my understanding why IDG have not been shouting about this magnificent whiskey from the rooftops.

Tasting Notes – Gilbey's bottling

From Bow Street Distillery. 40% abv

Nose Signs of great age: lots of woody notes mingling with the strong pot still. The oakiness comes out on top. Exceptionally weighty and when warmed enough in the hand, reveals the ripeness of a fruit pudding. But there is a misplaced mustiness and a vagueness about its true character.

Taste Soft malt arrives first, then an over-the-top oakiness followed by a very warming spicy attack. Some menthol in there, maybe?

Finish The wood now takes over completely. There is a charcoal-liquorice bitterness one normally finds in over-matured bourbon. A brief, sweet, toffee effect passes and then the wood returns for a very dry finale.

Comment Sometimes you come across a whiskey that you can tell was once great and has seen better days. This is one. It is obvious that the whiskey had been matured too long in the wood and extracted some of the less attractive oils. Still drinkable, and it's not without its pleasant moments, especially early on, but best kept in a cabinet somewhere as a aged example of one of Ireland's great, but now departed, whiskeys.

Tasting Notes – Irish Distillers' bottling

From Midleton Distillery

Nose   Stupendous nose; a bit of nip and bite but the sheer brittleness of the pot still is so real and alive you feel you could snap it in two. The malt also comes through alongside an apple-like fruitiness and a hovering trace of sherry, too. Every bit as clean as the old Redbreast is musty.

Taste   Just a sip is enough to fill your mouth with a multi-layered attack of malt and pepper plus a few sherry notes with the Irish pot still character arriving on the second wave and refusing to budge. This is enormously assertive stuff.

Finish   Very long indeed, and the late spice comes as the perfect ending to the great complexity of all that has gone on before. Although there is a dryness, some honey and fudge character also makes itself known and makes this whiskey more dangerously delectable than any other apart from Powers and possibly Green Spot.

Comment   This is a marvellous whiskey which should be better known. The pot still character gives an enormous depth and each time you taste it another little facet of its make-up is spotted. Although a perfect after-dinner and late night whiskey, I've enjoyed this during the day, too. Wonderful.

ROYAL IRISH

Distillery History

Question: what have the the downstairs bar of The Elk in Dundonald, Distillery Football Club, a park in Ulster's capital and the few bottles of 1951 Royal Irish whiskey which are still on sale, have in common? Answer: they are all that is left of the old Dunville's Royal Irish Distillery, one the greatest names in Ulster if not Irish whiskey.

The history books will tell you the Royal Irish Distillery made its last spirit in the late 1930s. But some older supporters of Distillery FC I met at their New Grosvenor Stadium at Lisburn, just outside Belfast, remember it working into the 50s, a claim backed up by a single cask of 1951 pot still found in a warehouse and now on offer in bottled form.

Dunville was for a great many years a Belfast whiskey and enjoyed a very high reputation. The family firm started off as blenders and in 1869 built Belfast's first commercial distillery just off the Grosvenor Road, and did not do the job by half. It was a massive structure, the company clearly setting their stall out as major players in the whiskey game. But to build the distillery at all the Dunville family had to carry out a bit of legal jiggerypokery and find a loophole in the law. In those days distillers were not allowed to deal in spirits, other than their own, unless outside a two mile radius from their distilleries. To overcome that hurdle two companies were set up: William Dunville & Co, distillers, and Dunville & Co, spirit dealers.

Even though the plant was a large one it continued to expand, winning gold medals at every exhibition it entered. It survived the First World War, the trade war following the emergence of the Irish Free State, and Prohibition in the USA where it had previously sold well, coming out of this trilogy of setbacks in a reasonably unscathed condition.

But just as they seemed set to relaunch into the USA in the mid 30s things started to go disastrously wrong. By that time the Dunville family connection had prematurely ended. When the elder statesman of the company, Robert Dunville died in 1910, his son, Colonel John Dunville, continued to run a tight company. He was eventually succeeded by his eldest son Captain Robert Dunville, but the firm was thrown into turmoil when, on a business trip to South Africa to secure further exports, Robert suddenly died. With his brother, John, having been killed during the First World War in an action for which he was posthumously awarded the Victoria Cross, there were no more Dunvilles to keep the flag flying.

The non-family board did not appear to have the same belief in the old company as the founding family. Despite having three pot stills and two grain stills, thus being self-sufficient enough to produce both blended and pure pot still whiskey, and owning the excellent Scottish distillery at Bladnoch in Dumfries and Galloway, they decided not to attack the American market. Instead, they approached the Scottish Distillers Company Ltd, inviting them to take them over. Their prospective buyers were not sufficiently interested, announcing that they had no faith in Irish whiskey.

Amazingly Dunville's wound themselves up, an action which shocked Belfast at the time and has never been fully explained by industrial historians. The company was, compared with many others at that time, in a healthy state of affairs. It appears, though, that some attempt was made to produce whiskey at the old distillery again in the 1950s but this was a short-lived and evidently unsuccessful bid to rekindle distilling in the city.

In 1879, just nine years after the building of the distillery was completed, workers from Dunville set up their own football team on a piece of land lent to them by the distillery. The club went on to win the Irish League just 17 years later and around the turn of the century were one of the most powerful clubs in Ireland.

Apart for a short spell in the 1920s when the expanding distillery tried to build on the site of the club's ground, only to find it was unsuitable, Distillery stayed at their Grosvenor Road ground until 1971. In 1963 the side played Benfica at Windsor Park in the European Cup. The game was switched from the Distillery because a bumper crowd was expected. But in monsoon conditions, only 17,000 attended — 3000 less than the Distillery ground capacity. Remarkably, the part-timers of Distillery held the reigning European champions to a 3-3 draw, with Tom Finney, famous for wearing the white of England and Preston, being brought out of retirement to play his only game for the club and wear the white of Distillery FC.

The ground was literally in the shadows of the grim, four-storey high, brick-built distillery. When it was constructed it was on the outskirts of the town and from the roof a dramatic view of the city and the countryside was offered. But by 1971 it found itself at the heart of the conflict around the Grosvenor Road. Although the club was one of only a handful to draw both its supporters and players from both Catholic and Protestant areas, the ground became the target of firebomb attacks. With sadness the old club moved to a greenfield site and another link was lost.

Some of you may remember seeing Dunville's whiskey quite recently. You did, but it was Scotch. The Dunville name was bought by Belfast wine and spirit merchant Philip Russell. He tried to do a deal with Irish Distillers to supply him with Irish whiskey, but they refused. Instead, he sold Dunville's as a Scotch whisky, only with an 'e'! He is currently holding talks with Cooley in the hope they will allow him to realise his dream of seeing Irishmen drink Dunville whiskey, made in Ireland once more.

His company also owns three bars, one of them The Elk. Downstairs is a glittering array of original Dunville mirrors and adverts he has managed to compile over the years. To visit the bar, it may be worth taking a little detour in Belfast and pass slowly along the spur road linking the M1 to M2. Because if you do, you will be driving just behind one of the goals where Distillery's ground used to be. And directly under your tyres will be the very spot where, for nearly 70 years, one of the finest of all Ireland's whiskeys was made in its steel-girdered still house, which is now merely a picture of vanished beauty.

ROYAL IRISH

Tasting Notes

From Wm Cadenhead. Distilled 1951. Bottled 1991. 66% abv

Nose Very soft indeed. Comes through like a very high class bourbon. No pot still character at all. A charming mixture of fruit, flowers and soft spices, but all rather non-specific. Tremendous.

Taste Sweet start, a quick malt burst, then the whiskey dies for a while. The wood is so intense it is unpleasant. Certainly the middle is taken up with concentrated wood juices rather than any barley, whether malted or not.

Finish This is the big surprise. As you hit the woody wall there does not appear to be any way through. Yet, on the other side, eventually some very clean and beautifully textured malt comes. Again it is sweet and hangs about the mouth.

Comment Oddly, during the Second World War, all the whiskey from the distillery was shipped to Campbeltown to avoid it being bombed. Yet the cask from which this whiskey came was discovered recently in a Belfast warehouse by a Campbeltown distiller! This is one of the most remarkable whiskeys I have ever tasted, anywhere in the world. How can something that noses so superbly and finishes with such style be so awful in the middle? A quite puzzling relic of Belfast's finest.

THREE STILLS IRISH SPIRITS

Distilled & bottled by
Irish Distillers Ltd.,
Bow Street Distillery
Smithfield Dublin 7.

30% vol.   Distributed by Fitzgerald & Co. Ltd.   700ml℮

Brand History

Launched to combat the ultra cheap spirits on the corner shop market this cannot be called whiskey since it contains only 30% abv. To qualify as Irish whiskey it must be at least 40% abv. The blend is selected from very light grains and some light pot still, all produced at Midleton.

Tasting Notes

Nose	Soft and uncomplicated: some pot still sweetness but not very clean or clear.
Taste	Quite lively for such a weak spirit. Obviously some very young whiskeys have been put in to pep it all up. The start, though, is rather oily and this unbalanced note stays throughout.
Finish	Oily and insignificant, the maltiness does

come through but there is still an over-whelming bitterness which suggests all is not well.

Comment This is designed at the low, budget end of the market and you get what you pay for. For the real Irish whiskey connoisseur this is one to grimace and splutter over.

Tullamore Dew

Distillery History

Straddling the banks of the narrow and gentle flowing River Clodagh, in the centre of a neat and friendly Offaly town, lie the crumbling remains of a distillery which in its day was one of the great whiskey centres of Ireland.

The distillery was once Tullamore which was founded by 1829 by a Michael Molloy, taking advantage of the closure of two other distilleries which had earlier operated in the town. Although a rival distillery was built soon after, Molloy's enterprise saw off that particular threat. The distillery, by no means the biggest in Ireland but enjoying a fine reputation, passed into the hands of nephew Bernard Daly in 1857, on Molloy's death. Thirty years later it was the turn of his son, Captain Bernard Daley to take control. But Capt Daley decided his life lay outside the whiskey industry and promoted the distillery's engineer, Daniel E. Williams, to the post of general manager.

Williams had been at the distillery since he was 15 and, very much unlike his employer, whiskey was in his blood and was his whole life. After Williams took control he persuaded Captain Daley to invest in expanding the plant. As Williams grew more powerful and Captain Daley's meagre interest in the distillery withered further, he managed to buy into the company, eventually taking overall control.

The distillery had success with their pot still whiskey which they marketed as Tullamore Dew. Williams had selected the brand name as a pun on his own initials. The name had a ring which appealed, as did the style of the whiskey which was a little lighter than the average Irish pot still. The advertising slogan: 'Give Every Man his Dew' became one of the best known in Ireland.

With Tullamore being located in the heart of the Irish midlands, where the roads were rutted and travel was slow and where steam was yet to arrive, the distillery thrived in its earliest days thanks to the Grand Canal which runs through the town. Coal was brought to the distillery from England and the same barges would then travel back, laden with whiskey. With the arrival of the railways, communications improved even further.

However, every convenient means of transportation counts for nothing if no one is buying your product and by the 1950s Tullamore Distillery, like many others in Ireland, was experiencing financial problems. The market had shrivelled considerably and the distillers looked to new horizons to rediscover success.

They hit upon the idea of producing a whiskey-based liqueur which they called Irish Mist. Daniel Williams had begun the search for a recipe in his day, but it was not until after the war that they discovered it in the most unlikely of circumstances. It is said Williams had heard about a traditional Irish drink called heather wine, its principal ingredients being Irish pot still whiskey, herbs and heather honey. But his researches came to nought as it appeared the secret had been taken to the continent over a century before. Sometime in 1948 an Austrian refugee visited the head office opposite the distillery and showed them a recipe similar to the one for which they were hunting. And that, legend has it, is how Irish Mist came into being, although today it is made by Cantrell & Cochrane, still in Tullamore, but using Scotch whisky as well as Irish.

Oddly, the success of Irish Mist sounded the death-knell to the old distillery which was becoming increasingly more expensive to operate and in need of more increasingly costly maintenance and upgrading. By 1954 they had more pot still whiskey than they knew what to do with and ceased production, never to start again.

Parts of the distillery can still be seen, but as this book was being researched, I witnessed some of the old warehouses being demolished. Tullamore practiced triple distillation and those stills can still be seen. They have been moved to an outside site at the Kilbeggan Distillery just down the road where they cut an impressive, though forlorn figure.

And the only dew they produce today forms on the outside, rather than the inside, when another morning dawns and they become an even more distant part of Irish distilling history.

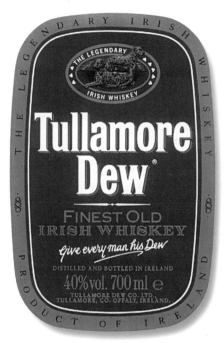

Brand History

While this blend has been ticking over in Ireland for the last few years, abroad it has achieved success out of all proportion to the quality of the whiskey. Being very light it has made a mark with those who prefer their whiskey not to occupy the tastebuds too much.

The early days of this whiskey have already been told since they were so closely knitted to the success of the old Tullamore Distillery. But 1993 can be seen as a watershed year for this whiskey since Irish Distillers allowed it to go to Cantrell & Cochrane, a company which themselves once hoped to own the Irish Distillers Group, rather than just one of its brands.

Tony O'Brien, C&C's managing director immediately announced bold plans for the brand: 'We intend to quickly establish Tullamore Dew in the core Irish whiskey market of Ireland, UK and the US and to further support it in its existing areas of strength.'

I suggested to him at the time that to gave it a taste, preferably of Irish pot still whiskey, might help this; or even make it the world's only internationally marketed pure pot still! But he pointed out that it is the top-selling Irish in Germany just the way it is. Of course, he's right, and this is the company's dilemma: with it selling so well in Germany, Denmark (where it is also the best selling Irish) and France, and seeing a 17°% growth in sales in 1993, do they leave it the way it is, or redesign its taste profile to make it unmistakably Irish? Or do they even introduce a super-premium brand with an age statement to put a greater emphasis on quality?

I, for one, will be watching and tasting Tullamore Dew with great interest in the forthcoming year or so.

Tasting Notes

Nose	The grainiest, least Irish of all popular Irish whiskeys; there is a begrudging pot still maltiness, but very faint.
Taste	Soft and light to the point that it is hard to detect this as an Irish whiskey. It is very sweet from the outset and some malt does assemble for the middle. But it is all terribly simple and lacking in any form of complexity.
Finish	There is a welcome wave of spiciness which lasts only a second or two and is replaced by a buttery smoothness and heaps of vanilla.
Comment	A semi-pleasant, untaxing whiskey which refuses to do anything which excites the palate. The sweetness can be attractive. But watch this one: drink it too cold and it can be rather astringent and harsh, and following the wrong kind of food it can be bitter and unyielding. Best drunk hand-warm and with a very clear palate. Only then does it reveal a limited charm. Now

in new hands, one hopes Cantrell & Cochrane will get together with Irish Distillers to pep this up.

Tasting Notes

From Wm Cadenhead. Distilled 1949. Bottled 1991. 65.6% abv

Nose Somehow or other some lingering, though fully stretched, traditional Irish pot still notes still hang around despite the encroaching bourbony woodiness. Light and very sweet.

Taste Sweet, extremely malty. More like a Scottish single malt than Irish pot still in its mouth feel and development. There is a quite superb honey middle which manages to shine and fend off a woodiness which has managed to stay in acceptable proportions.

Finish Quite delightful. Again the malt manages to come through with ease and clings pleasantly to the palate. That appealing sweetness also continues to deliver the goods. This comes in fruity form, perhaps even with hints of dried apple. Splendid.

Comment A real surprise this. Certainly not as good as when the original was in its finest fettle but the malt really is quite impressive and a fruitiness abounds. Very drinkable even today.

The Tyrconnell Single Malt

Distillery History

Dotted around Ireland are a number of peculiarly-shaped buildings to which architects travel from all over the world to both inspect and sometimes admire. These buildings were designed and constructed in the inter-war years by one of their Czech colleagues. Their only purpose was to turn potato solids and waste into alcohol.

These strange buildings, an early monument to the ugliness created when concrete is combined with steel, are found in the most unlikely places in the Republic. It was the Dublin Government which actually commissioned their building and their severity is accentuated by the tranquillity of the settings in which they are found. I accidentally stumbled across one located in a small village not very far from Malin Head, Ireland's most northerly point. It was a near enough replica of the one I had already visited just north of Dundalk whose function in life today is not to distil from potatoes, but from malted barley. For this is now Ireland's third whiskey distillery: Cooley.

Considering the short time Cooley Distillery has been in operation it has had a pretty dramatic life. But its gestation was a long affair, going back to the early 1970s when an Irishman studying at Harvard University looked into, as part of his business degree, the marketing of Irish whiskey. As far as John Teeling was concerned, the Irish made the best whiskey in the world but had not the slightest clue how to market it.

It was around that time that IDG had taken over Bushmills and were trying desperately to get their product away from the bottom of a marketing trough. Teeling kept his distance from the industry until 1986 when it became an open secret that Irish Distillers were looking for a major buyer. He hovered around the scene on the off-chance that he could make a successful bid for the company, but in the end it was a larger, international, corporate fish which swallowed the prize.

The next step, therefore, was to set up his own

distilling company. He had to find other financial partners and when that was achieved he paid the Irish Government £120,000 for the Ceimici Teo Distillery at Dundalk which he immediately renamed Cooley. The buying of the distillery was the easy bit: a further £3m was spent in turning it into a whiskey distillery complete with pot and patent stills.

The distillery also needed some famous names to help sell their new product when it had matured. So they then acquired both the John Locke's and Tyrconnell brand names. In 1989 the production of both malt and grain whiskey began. For three years the distillery produced vast amounts of spirit, using the warehouses which once stored whiskey at the old Kilbeggan Distillery and at Tullamore.

The arrival of Cooley was seen as nothing less than a commercial annoyance by Irish Distillers since it cut directly across their plan to control the marketing of all whiskey produced in Ireland. By 1992 Cooley was experiencing serious cash flow problems and were looking for a white knight to buy the company. A number of Scottish distillers looked at Cooley but shook their heads rather than their potential partners' hands.

But Irish Distillers could not ignore the 44,000 casks of spirit maturing into Irish whiskey which had been stockpiled in those warehouses. Nor the fact that The Tyrconnell Single Malt had been launched onto the market and at least one blend was on its way. Irish Distillers mounted a £22 million takeover bid for Cooley, a move which was welcomed by those who wanted to get some return on the £10 million which had been invested in the project. But a rather unfair criticism of the quality of Cooley whiskey, backed up by Irish Distillers' known intention of closing the distillery down, meant that those directly involved in its production were keen to keep Cooley if not independent, then certainly out of the hands of Pernod-Ricard, Irish Distillers' owners.

Although Irish Distillers actually bought some of Cooley's stocks to help keep the company afloat while the powers that be made up their minds, the takeover was never to go ahead. It was finally scuppered by the Competitions Authority of the Irish Government, even after appeal.

Today Cooley is still looking for a company which can guarantee its future by injecting enough money to start those pot stills again. But at least in the meantime its outlook seems brighter having agreed deals with powerful companies like Guinness in Northern Ireland, Moet-Hennessy in France and Heaven Hill Distillers in the USA to act as agents.

Brand History

The Tyrconnell is a proud name which conjures up many different images of Ireland. The romantic may recall the ancient Celtic kingdom once located in the remote north-west of Ireland by that epithet, or the sportsman may remember reading about the horse of that name which won the Irish Classic, the Queen Victoria Plate in 1876 at odds of 100-1, or, more likely today, it might just be the whiskey which comes most readily to mind.

In 1992 the single malt whiskey from Cooley Distillery was bottled and sold under that title for the first time. This may have been Cooley's debut, but The Tyrconnell brand was far from new. It was one of the main whiskeys made at the Derry Distillery of A.A. Watt (a family company which had owned the legendary horse) and was sold successfully as pure pot still in the USA.

The distillery was on the brink of closure by the early 1920s and the death of Andrew Watt, ironically the result of a hunting accident, allowed the Distillers Company Limited of Scotland to move in and buy the concern in 1922 and close it three years later. The distillery, like many others in Ireland, was also badly hit by prohibition in the States and the trade war between the new Irish Free State and the UK. The Watt family, now without a distillery, then formed a blending company which continued to market The Tyrconnell, but that too closed in 1970.

The current Tyrconnell is a vatting of three and four-year-old malts. Its very first bottling had been too dependent on early, experimental whiskeys and was not too pleasant. However, top Scottish blender Billy Walker of Burn Stewart Distillers had been brought in to iron out some initial distilling difficulties. On his

THE

TYRCONNELL

★ ★ ★

◆ S I N G L E M A L T ◆

Tyrconnell wins! 100 tol.

PURE POT STILL

IRISH WHISKEY

DISTILLED MATURED AND BOTTLED IN IRELAND BY
ANDREW A. WATT & CO.
RIVERSTOWN DUNDALK IRELAND.

ESTABLISHED 1762

70 cl ℮   PRODUCT OF IRELAND   40% vol

suggestion Cooley even produced a very heavily peated Irish whiskey, which, with a phenolic content of 25 parts per million, is as heavy as some Scottish island and Islay whiskies. Today The Tyrconnell is delicious: a consistently better malt which has been vatted by legendary Scottish blender Jimmy Lang, once of Chivas Bros, who compares Cooley whiskey to a high class Scottish Lowland malt whisky. Beware, though, the occasional old sub-standard bottling.

Its markets are Holland, Switzerland, Northern Ireland, USA, France, Germany and the UK where a Cooley single malt will be available as an own-brand in one of the supermarket chains.

Tasting Notes

Nose   There is a depth, maturity and complexity
             here, way beyond the four years this whis-
             key has been in the cask. The nose is a

131

beguiling cross between a northern Highland citrus-spiciness and a honey-lightness seen in some southern Perthshire Scottish malts. Yet despite that, this is an all-malt whiskey which retains an unmistakable Irishness. Very full, enticing and fruity.

Taste   Fills the mouth with a well-structured viscosity on which hang those same honeyed notes noticeable on the nose. A tang of oranges, also. The malt is very strong throughout and balances well with the oily sweetness. Delightful.

Finish   Quite long, with some drying effect and the malt becomes quite dominant without the soft fruits and honey which helped make up the middle. There is perhaps a slight, youthful off-note towards the very end, but it is a minor blemish.

Comment   When this malt was first launched its quality was variable to say the least. Beware of the early bottlings which contained some very poor whiskeys. However, for the last year The Tyrconnell has been nothing short of a revelation and a delight. This is now a very accomplished whiskey at such a young age and one which should appeal to both sexes. As the brand gets older, so too will the whiskeys used and the finish will improve. Exciting times ahead.

LIQUEURS

Whether you are sheltering from the near 100°F heat of California with an Irish Coffee in the Buena Vista Cafe, or hiding from icy February winds which rip along the River Liffey by ducking into a bar for a Hot Powers, you are taking solace in an Irish Liqueur.

A Hot Whiskey, where boiling water and brown sugar are added to the Irish of your choice (often a Power's), is perhaps the oldest tradition of a liqueur in Ireland. Irish Coffee is still universally popular, in the States in particular , but it is another liqueur altogether which has taken the world by storm: Baileys. The latest figures released by the Dublin company are enough to make the cream curdle for every other liqueur company in business. Of all Irish beverage exports, Baileys accounts for 47%; the brand now makes up a full 1% of Ireland's entire export trade; it stands 15th in the world's top selling spirits, now selling in no fewer than 160 countries.

Not bad for a drink which was launched as recently as 1974 by Gilbey's to an intially underwhelming response by critics in the trade. The following year saw just 20,000 cases sold, failing even to get into the British market. In 1992 case sales stood at 3.8 million: Baileys is regarded as *the* marketing success story of Ireland, a phenomenon which happens once in a businessman's lifetime.

The liqueur is produced at a brand new plant on an industrial estate just off the Naas Road on the outskirts of Dublin where both the mixing of the ingredients and the bottling take place.

The development of the drink was a pretty commonsense affair. Gilbey's wanted to create a real Irish image for the brand and so combined the two things for which the country was famous and of which there was a bountiful supply: fresh cream and whiskey. The difficulty came in what the make-up and mix of other ingredients would be. Cocoa, although hardly Irish, seemed another natural choice but the other ingredients remain secret, and wild horses won't drag the information from them.

Originally the liqueur had a shortish shelf life. No additives are put in to extend Baileys' longevity but, during the manufacturing process, they have found a way which alters the molecular structure of some of the ingredients so that when they are combined with the natural preservative qualities of alcohol, a life of 18 months can now be achieved.

It was no surprise when other companies followed suit in trying to create an Irish whiskey cream liqueur to bolster their own fortunes, but so far none has succeeded with anything like the ease of Baileys.

R. & J. Emmet and Co was formed in 1980 and from its Bailieboro plant in Co. Cavan launched Emmets Classic Irish Cream and Dubliner Irish Cream among others. None managed quite to achieve the all-round complexity of Baileys, although they did build up a healthy enough trade in North America and Europe for Baileys to take them over in October 1991.

There are even cream liqueurs containing Irish whiskey and spirit coming in from Holland, such as Millwood. In all cases the whiskey is supplied by Irish Distillers, but it appears to me that none can match the quality of the blend used by Baileys. It is malt-dominant with pot still which is mainly aged about three and a half years with some four and five-year-olds thrown in. The grain is just under four years old. It is hard not to believe that this is one of the main reasons for Baileys' depth of character.

Before the Baileys' success story, the premium Irish liqueur had been Irish Mist (see Tullamore), although even this dated back to only just after the Second World War. However, this was before the era of the cream-based dominance and although available in 80 countries, its worldwide sales of 80,000 cases hardly stand comparison with Baileys. Irish Mist's owners Cantrell & Cochrane again moved swiftly into the cream liqueur sector with Carolans in 1978 and is now the second-largest selling liqueur of its genre with 600,000 annual cased sales. And like Baileys it launched a lighter version of their liqueur (which tastes very similar, just less intense and viscous) to appeal to the warmer climes of the States and with 50% less fat for the more health conscious.

BAILEYS

From Gilbey's, a subsidiary of IDV. 17% abv

Nose Still the sexiest, most complex of all Ireland's cream liqueurs. The spirit does show early but is swamped by rich cream and citrus fruit, pineapples, other tropical fruits and mint.

Taste Luxurious mouth feel, the chocolate cream makes the first stand but then a complex fruitiness joins forces with the Irish whiskey. No other cream liqueur allows the alcohol to muscle in, in such big fashion.

Finish Clinging and very long. Of all the Irish cream liqueurs this is the one which really shows whiskey in its teeth. There is a quite dry sub-stratum, too.

Comment Nothing like as sweet as other cream liqueurs. Very rich and unquestionably the unconquered champion of its type due to its complexity and power.

135

CAROLANS IRISH CREAM LIQUEUR

Tasting Notes

From TJ Carolan & Son, a subsidiary of Cantrell & Cochrane. 17% abv

Nose   Powerful caramel and crème brulée. Some alcoholic notes about, but nothing particularly Irish.

Taste   A rather uncomplicated smooth, cream-toffee and caramel beginning gives way to a pleasant, warming — almost spicy — middle.

Finish   Continues in this alcoholic mode for a few seconds before giving way to what had already gone before. Very creamy and undemanding.

Comment   Pleasant, but hardly for the sophisticate. All rather two-dimensional with cream-toffee and caramel on the one hand and alcohol on the other. It's marked as 'Irish Spirit'; certainly nothing to grab the whiskey lover here.

THE DUBLINER

Tasting Notes

From The Dubliner Liqueur & Spirit Co, a subsidiary of IDV. 17% abv

Nose   One of the most intriguing of all Ireland's cream liqueurs. There appears to be citrus and raisiny fruit with a sprig of spearmint. The chocolate-cream does not come through as being well-defined.

Taste   The alcohol comes through quickly leaving a coolness on the mouth, rapidly replaced by rich, milk chocolate.

Finish   A chocolate-orange effect clings around the palate for some time.

Comment   Difficult one to describe. On the nose it reminds me of a milk-shake I used to have on my first ever visit to the States as a child. There is something alien to the chocolate-creaminess we are used to in the UK. It also smells of freshly baked Maryland Cookies. It's never quite so interesting once on the palate, but a must for chocoholics. So I admit it: I like it!

137

EMMETS CLASSIC CREAM

Tasting Notes

From R. & J. Emmet, a subsidiary of IDV. 17% abv

Nose Cream, chocolate and orange. Very little whiskey noticeable.

Taste Much more relaxed than Baileys with none of the complexity. Not as sweet as some cream liqueurs, though sweet enough. Fruity, citrousy notes filter through.

Finish Low-key, creamy, chocolatey and oily. Again, not over complex.

Comment Enjoyable but possessing none of the multi-layered bite which makes Baileys exceptional

IRISH MIST

From The Irish Mist Co, a subsidiary of Cantrell & Cochrane. 35% abv

Nose A quite delicious balance here: at last some real whiskeys can be picked out. Not only can I detect Irish in there, I'd put my mortgage on there being some Scotch whisky too, probably Lowland. Against that is a rather sugary aroma holding together some very delicate herbs, spices and honey. Really very enjoyable, indeed.

Taste Immediately warming on the palate: a whole armada of spices sails across the mouth assaulting the tastebuds in a quite charming manner. The whiskey makes an impressive entrance, too. Despite the masking, rich, honey I still get a certain Scottishness to this; but if you search deep enough with your palate the Irishness shows up quite well, too.

Finish A subtle mixture of sweet and dry, the dryness lingering longest. It is hard to pick out the exact character: perhaps it is ginger, even with hints of burnt sugar.

Comment A real liqueur this. You can spend hours puzzling over what your tastebuds are trying to tell you. Extremely complex, sweet, but never cloyingly so, and a very impressive dry fade-out. The label claims there is heather-honey in here and I know what they mean. The whiskey character has a Scottish-Irishness. I'm sure they know what I mean. Really tasty: excellent.

MEADOW CREAM

Tasting Notes

From Halewood Vintners, a subsidiary of Pernod-Ricard. 14.5% abv. The base is claimed to be 'a blend of Dutch cream, white wine and Irish Whiskey'.

Nose   A fudgy sweetness and wine hangs well together. The spirit is quite shy.

Taste   Quite thin for a cream liqueur but despite the sweetness it does possess a certain nutty complexity and even a hint of herbs. Certainly the wine appears to have a bigger say than the spirit.

Finish   Sweet cream fudge, semi-oily and lingering.

Comment   If you have a sweet tooth and enjoy fudgy chocolates, or knows someone who does, you are on a winner here. The Irish whiskey, from Midleton, is barely noticeable on the nose, disappears completely on the palate and makes a pretty feeble appearance at the finish. The wine is much more dominant.

MILLWOOD WHISKEY CREAM

Tasting Notes

From Halewood Vintners, a subsidiary of Pernod-Ricard. 14.5% abv

Nose Deeper, more intense and less sweet than Meadow Cream, a gentle hint of tangerines with a soft spirit follow through.

Taste Full-bodied, much sweeter than the nose suggests. Again rather fudgy, only more spirit is evident than in Meadow Cream

Finish Begins sweet with a hint of praline which fades and becomes slightly dry. There is a strong viscosity throughout. Fruity notes come through at the last; the whiskey which had been lost without trace makes a grainy cameo appearance for a few moments close to the end.

Comment A pretty straight up-and-downer, this, not unlike a milk-shake in some ways. Little complexity but lots of oiliness which allow the liqueur to last

O'DARBY IRISH CREAM LIQUEUR

Tasting Notes

From J.J. O'Darby, a subsidiary of Gilbey's. 17% abv

Nose   Straight up-and-down: caramel, cream and chocolate with a non-specific alcohol buzz.

Taste   Thin compared to some, but pleasantly textured with an initial fruit and cream feel giving way to toffee.

Finish A bit like rich butter toffee helped along by a gentle spirit bite. Quite long and when the chocolate comes in, becomes surprisingly moreish.

Comment Not a high quality liqueur like Baileys and lacking anything bordering on complex. But if you like cream toffees you might find this quite interesting.

IRISH COCKTAILS

GRIT COCKTAIL
Half a jigger (1°fl oz/40ml) Irish whiskey. Half a jigger of Italian vermouth. Shake, then strain into a cocktail glass.

IRISH COLLINS
Fill goblet with fine ice. Juice of a small lemon. One spoon of powdered sugar. One jigger of Irish whiskey. Strain into large, thin glass and fill with one bottle of soda. Stir with spoon.

IRISH WHISKEY COOLER
One lemon rind. One jigger Irish whiskey. One pint of club soda. One dash Angostura Bitters. Serve in tall glass.

IRISH WHISKEY FIZZ
Juice of ° lemon. One barspoon of sugar. One jigger of Irish whiskey. Shake, strain into fizz glass. Fill glass from soda syphon.

IRISH ROSE HIGHBALL
One jigger Irish whiskey. One-third jigger of Grenadine syrup. One lump of ice. Fill glass from soda syphon.

IRISH ROSE
As above with 3 or 4 dashes of Grenadine syrup.

IRISH WHISKEY PUNCH
Juice of ° lemon. One barspoonful sugar. One jigger Irish whiskey. Shake and strain into goblet with crushed ice. Dress with fruit.

IRISH WHISKEY RICKEY
Juice of ° lime. One lump of ice. Add Irish whiskey to taste. Fill glass with carbonated mineral water. Stir with spoon.

IRISH WHISKEY SOUR
Juice of ° lemon. One barspoon of sugar. One jigger of Irish whiskey. Shake. Strain into sour glass. Dress with fruit.

IRISH SLING
In an old-fashioned glass, mix one jigger of gin, one jigger Irish whiskey. Crush one lump of sugar and two lumps of ice and add to glass.

POTEEN

The word in the glen says there is plenty of 'the stuff' about just now. The stuff, to the Irish, means only one thing: poteen.

Poteen or poitín (but always pronounced *potcheen*) is an Irish spirit which is a direct descendant of illegally distilled whiskey. It isn't whiskey anymore: not so much because it is never matured the three years required to make it so — that's the rule for Parliament whiskey — but because these days it's nearly impossible to find an illicit distiller who sticks exclusively to grain in the making of his prized, colourless fluid.

It was not too hard for me to track down a latter-day poteen maker when I was last in Ireland. That was partly because he was as keen to talk to a real, live whisky writer as I was see a secret craftsman at work. These days if you want some of the real stuff you have to ask a friend of a friend. Sixty years ago H.V. Morton, whose travel writing was a cross between William Cobbett's and Michael Palin's, discovered poteen with an old man in Co. Cork who let him have some only after Morton had told him, 'Mike O'Flaherty's black cow has died on him.' The asking price was nine shillings a bottle even in 1930; today it costs around seven or eight punts, sometimes even more. But at least you don't have to remember coded messages.

The poteen maker has a very special place in the hearts of the Irish and today's proper illicit distillers, as opposed to those who mass produce very poor quality stuff by adulterating it with meths, are viewed with a national pride that goes deep into Ireland's psyche. It all began on Christmas Day, 1661 when the English-based government slapped a tax of fourpence a gallon on all whiskey made. The number of illicit distillers increased by alarming proportions over the following centuries as the tax continued to rise and the lot of the Irish peasant worsened drastically.

It is all too easy to romanticise this period when a genuinely suppressed nation displayed their contempt for their lords by taking to the hills, bogs and glens to produce a whiskey which not only generated some much needed cash for its makers, but also was a welcome escape for the tens of thousands who drank it in Ireland's countless shebeens. And although poteen has earned its rightful place in Irish folklore, it was a feature of brutal times. While there was some fun and an understandable sense of achievement and victory over the authorities each time a drop from those mobile stills crossed an Irishman's lips, there was a very much darker side to it as well.

The duty on a gallon of whiskey had been raised to one shilling and tuppence by 1785 and to help finance the Napoleonic Wars, it was raised again to a numbing six shillings and a penny ha'penny in 1815. It was then that illicit distillation in Ireland was at its height, and the battle against it at its most bloody.

The Government sent soldiers out to aid the Excise authorities in suppressing illicit distillation. The most extraordinary contemporary account I have been able to find sits in the Public Records Office of Northern Ireland. They are the letters of an officer in the army, Samuel Lumsden, to members of his family back in England. His observations show just how whiskey and the plight of the Irish were so inextricably intertwined. He wrote on April 15th, 1816:

> In a detachment with another officer and 32 men 20 miles from Derry....except Potatoes and Eggs we cannot get an article of subsistence nearer than headquarters. Out every night searching for private Stills and generally not in vain....illicit distillation appears their only means of subsistence and yet the fines arising from it have actually ruined them.
>
> They are now desperate ... If another law of felony is imposed (illicit distillation) will be found insufficient to stop ... for transportation cannot deter men who are conscious their situation may be better but cannot be worse. The voice of kindness is so great a stranger to their ear that the first word of it awakens their utmost gratitude.

And on August 6th, 1816:

> I entered (this country) with a disposition to esteem the inhabitants but this atrocious

Murder (of Norton Butler of Grouse Hall, Carndonagh) has jaundiced my mind against the Bastardy of Scotch craft and Irish ferocity ... His murder was marked with particular ferocity ... after the two balls had entered him ... the fellow rushed forward and put his bayonet through his thigh entering four inches into the ground. In the struggle the bayonet broke and left him pinioned to the ground ... His death was occasioned by his exertion to put down illicit distillation ... the murderer is known and protected by the inhabitants and though the rewards for his detection are large, yet nothing will induce the infamous Crew to give him up. I was all last night searching for him.

A few days since I went out on Revenue duty with a Mr Callaghan, Surveyor of Excise. He and a gauger galloped after a man who was running off with a still. They left my view ... (twenty minutes later) I found Mr Callaghan to all appearances dead, his skull fractured with stones and entirely unable to speak or move.

This country is ruined, it is the station of Poverty — all who can are flying from the approaching ruin and hope in America to find hope and plenty.

Norton Butler had been one of the most active law agents in the battle against illicit distilling and before Lumsden's gruesome discovery, previous attempts had been made upon his life. The area Lumsden and Butler had been trying to police was located in Inishowen, the most northern tip of Donegal, close to Malin Head and a region which enjoyed a reputation in regard to Irish whiskey as Glenlivet did in the Scottish Highlands. A few years earlier in Inishowen, Aeneas Coffey, who later went on to become both Inspector General of Excise and the inventor of a continuous still which bears his name to this day, narrowly escaped with his life after a north Donegal illicit distilling militia set about him with such venom he was fortunate to live and achieve later fame. He recalled that 'they fractured my skull, left my body one mass of contusion, and gave me two bayonet wounds, one of which completely perforated my thigh. I owed my life to the rapid approach of the military party from which I had imprudently wandered a few hundred yards...'

Thankfully it has been many years since such horrors awaited those whose job it was to put down illicit distilling and today are totally unheard of. Where the British soldier and government agent failed, two major events helped reduce this traffic in Ireland. One was the extraordinary zeal of the temperance campaigner Father Mathew and the other was the gradual decline of the peasant status with more people being allowed to own their own land. Able to produce cash crops rather than whiskey, many former illicit distillers decided on a more legal way of life as Victorian Christian values and expectancy hardened.

At the time of Lumsden the poteen distilled was whiskey, or would have been had it been allowed to mature. Then it was drunk as many days or weeks old as it is now years. One of the biggest problems, though, was the making of the malt. It was common for the illicit distiller to leave a sack of grain in a stream, hoping it would not be detected, and allow it to dry in various places about his home, even under his bed if it had legs. Because of peat being used almost exclusively in the quick drying of the malt, any whiskey produced in Ireland with a peaty aroma and taste was called 'poteen-flavoured'.

Because of the time and trouble involved in the malting process potatoes became more commonly used by illicit distillers and in the 1880s molasses was found more than useful on account of the fact that it helped produce fermentable solids.

The stuff made by the poteen maker I visited in the mountains of Donegal, the perpetual heartland of illicit distilling, was based on just that. Today there is perhaps more hooch made in Galway than any other part of Ireland but it is all similar to my man's. He used to use an old copper still. Now, like others, he uses a Burco boiler. 'Cheap to run, twice as efficient.' Although the boiler is stainless steel, vitally, the condensing coil is still made of copper. But even here the distiller is keeping tradition alive in a way: last century Irish tinkers used to sell stills made from tin.

His recipe consists of two stones of unmalted barley, four stones of brown sugar, a gallon of treacle, a gallon of syrup, a box of apples to help fermentation and add flavour and a pound of yeast.

Where once the game of the distiller could be given away by the small plume of smoke which would rise from his bothy like a beacon into the sky, these days he has to be careful of his suppliers. Many an illicit distiller has been turned in by a shopkeeper in return for a small reward. This Donegal distiller gets his materials from trusted friends. In return they receive a bottle or two of the stuff.

What he makes is a lot better than the poteen I have tasted from other illicit distillers in Ireland. He has triple-distilled it, so although fiery, it remains light and soft with a fruitiness which possibly derives from the apples. Another curious link with the past here: it has been thought possible that a cider brandy may have been made in Ireland in the Middle Ages when a number of cider makers from Gloucestershire emigrated across the Irish sea.

The still is in a tiny ante-room off the kitchen and his entire output for a year is little more than 20 bottles. You will not find it on the duty-free shelves of Cork and Dublin airports like one 'poteen' from Bunratty Mead & Co, whose owner, Oliver Dillon, claims to produce the world's only commercial poteen in County Clare. Although the company cannot sell it in the Republic, the fact the Irish Government takes money off the distiller in taxation from his profits, somehow runs contrary to the spirit of the spirit!

Commercial enterprises apart, there is currently a renaissance of totally illegal poteen making in Ireland with, for example, illicit stills working out of Cork and Dublin, cities where they had long been extinct. But no one has any real idea just how many poteen makers are on the loose. The distiller up on his small holding in Donegal told me he knows four others, and those four probably know four others and so on. 'Don't you see,' he points out, 'it's not just a case of keeping the tradition alive. It's more the keeping of the tradition of sticking two fingers up to the authorities for not letting us do what all Irishmen consider a God-given right.'

BUNRATTY EXPORT POTCHEEN

Tasting Notes

40% abv

Nose In some ways nearer to poteen than new spirit from large stills, there is an odd, sugary sweetness which clings about the grain. It does lack the behind-the-counter poteen fruitiness and harshness, but is still very pleasant.

Taste Very sweet, grainy and quite full-tasting with a slight oiliness. By comparison, poteen I tasted in the hills attacks the tongue and roof of the mouth without mercy and leaves a more complex, though usually less smooth residual feel.

Finish Thinnish for poteen but with a pleasant spiciness which peps it all up. The malt effect is rather single-layered.

Comment A sanitised but still moderately enjoyable version of the stuff you find from nameless friends of friends. It would be better at full strength, though, as this is rather too soft. Available from duty-free in Ireland and even from Fortnum & Mason in London's Piccadilly.

A LATE 19TH-CENTURY POTEEN MAKER AT HIS STILL

WHERE TO VISIT

D on't be put off by the fact that there are only three distilleries in Ireland, one of which, Cooley, is not currently in production. At Midleton however, the Jameson Heritage Centre is now attracting thousands of visitors from all over the world in a similar fashion to Old Bushmills, the only working distillery in Ireland to welcome people with open arms.

But in fact, Ireland is a little green gem for the whisk(e)y enthusiast. It may have only the one working distillery to inspect but it boasts two ancient distilleries, one at Midleton, the other at Kilbeggan, which date from the late 18th and early 19th centuries, each preserved in aspic. They have a charm and sense of history and have no peers anywhere else in the world.

Old Bushmills, Co Antrim, Northern Ireland

Open all year, Mondays to Thursdays, 0900-1200 & 1330-1530 and on Fridays, 0900-1145. Entry £2.

✆ 02657-31521.

Bushmills is found on the north Antrim coast, just two miles from the eighth natural wonder of the world, the Giant's Causeway, part of a series of peculiar geological features formed by the cooling of volcanic basalt rock. The Antrim coast is one of the most glorious and least-known treasures of the British Isles and its softly sculpted hills and mountains, which lie just inland, are well worth a visit before or after your tour of the distillery.

The Old Bushmills Distillery stands proud and classical, its twin fishscale-tiled pagodas marking where the malting once took place, are as much a focal point to the old works as floodlight pylons are to a soccer stadium. The distillery annually welcomes over 70,000 people and has become one of Northern Ireland's biggest attractions. This year the building of its new visitor's centre was completed, with a former warehouse being converted into a reception area before guided tours. These invariably finish with a glass of 10-year-old malt or the masterful Black Bush in a bar beside the museum which holds relics from not only Bushmills, but also the lost distillery of Coleraine.

The Irish Whiskey Corner, Bow Street, Dublin

Daily tours, Monday to Friday, 1530. In summer, extra tour at 1100, May to October. Entry £3.

℃ (01)872-5566

Taking up part of what remains of a warehouse attached to the old Jameson Bow Street Distillery, is The Irish Whiskey Corner. Owned, developed and recently completed by Irish Distillers, it is next door to their current head office and is the only place in Eire's capital which has been given over to the country's long and proud distilling tradition.

Outside it is a still from the Power's distillery, and another, which once hissed and steamed within the Bow Street complex, is inside. The centre is part-museum and part-exhibition with a dummy cooper and cut-out maltmen giving some idea of how whiskey is made. There are also mounted photographs showing the history of Jameson's Bow Street Distillery and an audio-visual centre to take people through the whiskey-making process. And, of course, there is the Ball O'Malt bar, where, after one of the conducted tours, you will be allowed to sample a range of whiskeys from around the world in order to educate your palate to the joys of drinking Irish.

It is certainly an enjoyable place to spend an hour and learn something about Ireland's distilling heritage. And while at Bow Street, and if you are not squeamish, it is worth enquiring to see if you can gain access to the famous crypt of St Michan's Church, where the strange subterranean microclimate has ensured that the corpses have remained in a mummified state for many centuries. This is where Alfred Barnard began his journey of Ireland's distilleries in 1885; it was a place of great reknown, even over a century ago.

The Jameson Heritage Centre, Midleton, Co Cork

Daily tours from mid-March to end October, 1000-1800. Entry £3.50 (£1.50 for children). Group rates available.

✆ (021) 613594

Just 13 miles east of Cork city this newly-opened facility gives a complete picture of the making of Irish whiskey. There are plenty of artefacts to interest the whiskey-lover, including a 40ft waterwheel and the largest pot still in the world.

Money is being spent on making it easier for people to walk around the site; in so doing I just hope they don't fill in a rut which is found below a very low level bridge. That rut was formed over a period of 70 years by distillery workmen riding their bikes under the bridge, to and from work, and ducking to their handlebars. If they got the line wrong a nasty crack on the head was a guaranteed certainty.

Elsewhere around the old distillery grounds multilingual audio-visual booths have been set up to tell people in which part of Midleton they have found themselves. The tourist attractions are far more high-tech than the distillery ever was. Back inside the distillery is the only bar I know which stocks every brand of whiskey made by the company, including the sherry-rich Distillery Reserve, a heavyweight 12-year-old. It cannot be bought anywhere else.

It will be interesting to see if Irish Distillers make the new Midleton Distillery equally as accessible to the public as the old one. There are no plans as yet, but watch this space.

Kilbeggan, Tullamore and Monasterevan

I have already devoted a section of this book to the history of Locke's distillery at Kilbeggan. With the sun reflecting off the River Brosna, and the waterwheel dark against the distillery's 18th-century whitewashed wall, it is truly one of the most gladdening visions of Ireland. Inside the distillery are the same implements which were in use from the last century up until the distillery's demise in the 1950s. A trust has been set up to keep the buildings not only in this same breath-taking condition, but also to carry out whatever restoration work is possible. There are hopes the waterwheel will again be driving some of the machinery and plant which still lie dusty, redundant but resplendent within the distillery.

From Kilbeggan it is just a six-mile drive to Tullamore where the remains of the old distillery can still be seen. South-east from Kilbeggan and away from the direction of Cork is another gem, Monasterevan Distillery. Barnard accompanied his description of the distillery with a drawing. The main body of the offices are so well-preserved today, that I found I was able to drive up and park beside it without any confirmation from the locals that I had found the right place.

The inside of the distillery, containing some of the most extraordinary and beautiful industrial architecture in Ireland, is on private land behind a shop and not open to public access. But although the distillery has been silent since 1921, you can still make out much from Barnard's drawing, including Brennan's Bar which, typically for Ireland, doubles up as a store which you have to walk through before you get to the serious bit. But it is another Monasterevan bar, Mooney's, on Main Street, effectively the Tullamore road, which is most sought after by the whiskey lover. In a well-locked cabinet inside the snug is a bottle of Monasterevan from the last century, unopened and full of golden promise. It is the last remaining bottle of Monasterevan known to exist.

But for something that is just too special to miss, it has to be Kilbeggan. Owned by a trust, it is one of Irish whiskey's 'neutrals'. True, part of the site is owned by Cooley Distillery, who have used the warehousing to mature their own make, and the stills of Tullamore, which can be seen from inside the distillery, belong to Cooley, too. As you gaze on this wonderful piece of history, you cannot help but feel that it belongs not just to Ireland, but to every man and woman from every whiskey distillery who, over the course of the last two centuries, spent their lives making Irish pot still whiskey, for many, *the* most glorious spirit in the world.

GLOSSARY OF TERMS

Alcohol: The compound which accumulates whenever yeast ferments. This is one of the major by-products of fermentation.

Aqua vitae: The Latin for 'water of life'. Usually distilled from wine, whiskey was also called this by clerics for the purposes of official documentation.

Blending: The process and craft of mixing malt or pot still whiskey with grain whiskey. In Scotland blended whisky will usually contain malts and grain from a great number of distilleries. But in Ireland all the whiskey may not only be from a single distillery, Midleton, but also from pot and column stills only.

Bond: The warehouse(s) in which whiskey stocks are held until Excise duty is levied upon them.

Brewing: The process of infusing cereal grains in hot water (mashing) which, with the aid of yeast (fermentation), produces alcoholic liquids (wash) from the dissolved sugars present.

Casks: A barrel which contains maturing spirit or whiskey. For spirit to mature into whiskey it must, by law, be kept in oak casks for a minimum of three years. The barrels are likely to have originally contained bourbon or sherry. The most common casks are butts of approximately 500 litres volume and hogsheads of between 250 and 305 litres volume.

Coffey still: A patent still invented by Aeneas Coffey allowing the continuous distillation of wash. (See also Column Still.)

Column still: Apparatus designed for the continuous production of alcoholic spirit. Spirit produced exclusively through these stills is, after three years maturation, called grain whiskey. Pot still whiskey is produced through these at Midleton Distillery as the distilling process in completed in pot stills.

Draff: The spent solids of cereal grain, or dregs, from the brewing process which are removed from the mash tun and usually sold on as a nutritious feed for farm livestock.

Feints: The impure spirit produced from the tail end of the second distillation, and which needs to be redistilled to make suitable for fillings.

Fermentation: The active period during the brewing process when the yellow-brown, sugar-rich liquid wort reacts with yeast. The liquid froths violently as both carbon dioxide and alcohol are produced. After about two to three days the liquid becomes still and is ready for distillation. The process is carried out in large holding vessels called wash backs.

Fermenters: An Irish term for wash backs.

Fillings: The term applied to new spirit filled into cask before being warehoused for maturation.

Foreshots: The oily spirit produced at the beginning of each run from the stills; unsuitable for filling, it is redistilled.

Gauger: The old name given to an exciseman, whose job it was to put down illicit distillation and smuggling.

Grain whiskey: Whiskey which has been produced from column stills, usually from wheat or maize but with a small amount of malted barley to aid fermentation.

Grist: The crushed grains which are placed in the mash tun. In the case of Irish pot still, a mixture of unmalted and malted barley which is added to hot water called liquor in the first step of the brewing process.

Malt: Barley which has been steeped in cold water then allowed to dry for several days, allowing germinating shoots to develop. During this period the starches inside the husk are modified to sugar-like carbohydrates. When the 'sugar' content is at its peak the barley is dried to prevent further germination.

Marrying: The period in which whiskies from more than one distillery or set of stills are allowed to react with each other to form a blend or a vatting before bottling. In Scotland this process sometimes takes months; in Ireland usually days.

Mashing: The process by which the grist is added to hot water in order to dissolve all the fermentable starches.

Mash tun: The large metal container in which grist is added to the liquor (hot water) for mashing to be carried out. The liquid formed is called wort.

Maturation: When spirit is placed into a cask, over a period of years it reacts with chemicals in the wood and with any sherry residue, to form its character. The longer the whiskey is kept in the wood the greater the influence of the wood will be. Whiskey only matures in wood, never in glass, so the age of a whiskey on the bottle shows the age of the youngest whiskey used at the time of bottling.

Mouth feel: The term applied to the effect a whiskey (or any other alcoholic drink) has on the palate. It could be smooth, fiery, soft, light, cloying and so on.

Patent still: See Coffey still.

Peat: A turf-like material formed by decaying organic, vegetable matter found in boggy land. When cut and dried it serves as a burning fuel. Traditionally used in the making of whiskey for the drying of malt. Islay whiskies in Scotland are particularly noted for the pungent spirit produced by the use of peat and once Ireland used it, too, especially in the making of illicit whiskey. There is currently no Irish whiskey on the market which contains peaty whiskey, although Cooley do have some maturing in their warehouses and it may be specially bottled at a later date.

Poteen (or poiteen): An illicit spirit once made from malted barley, sometimes from potato, but today is more likely to be made from molasses.

Pot still: Bulbous copper container in which the wash, produced from either pure malted barley or a mixture of malted and unmalted barley, is heated until vapours containing alcohol rise and separate from the heated liquids.

Pot still whiskey: The traditional name given to Irish whiskey which is made from a mixture of malted and unmalted barley. Once, it also contained small quantities of oats and rye. Not to be confused with single malt, or pure malt, both of which are also produced in pot stills.

Run: The colourless, alcohol-rich liquid, or spirit, which flows from the still after having passed through the condensing apparatus.

Shebeen: An illegal drinking house, usually located in the most desolate areas of Ireland, but also occasionally in towns. Here poteen is consumed and sometimes sold by the bottle.

Single malt: Malt whiskey produced from just one distillery and not mixed with either grain or pot still whiskey.

Uisce beatha: The Gaelic name meaning 'water of life', and the derivative term for whiskey and whisky: uisce was corrupted to uisgey and thus whiskey.

Vatting: The mixing together of identical styles of whiskey (i.e, pure malt, pot still etc) from the same distillery but from different casks. Not to be confused with a vatted whisky, which is a mixture of Scotch malt whisky but from more than one distillery.

Wash: The beer-like liquid which has undergone the fermentation process and is ready to be pumped into the wash still for the first distillation.

Wash back: Sometimes called fermenters in Ireland, they can be made from either wood, for example larch or pine, or stainless steel.

Wood: Almost certainly the most important single element in the maturation process. All whiskey in the major whiskey producing nations has to be matured, by law, in oak. See casks and maturation.

Worm: Traditionally the coiled copper tube in which the vaporised alcohols from the stills condense to form the spirit which matures into whiskey.

Wort: The liquid high in dissolved sugars which is cooled before being pumped into the wash backs for the next stage in brewing: fermentation.

Yeast: Tiny plant organisms which feed off sugar and create alcohol and carbon dioxide as by-products. Added to the wort in the mash tuns to aid fermentation.

BIBLIOGRAPHY

Barnard, Alfred; *The Whisky Distilleries of the United Kingdom* (London, 1887)

Bielenberg, Andrew; *Locke's Distillery: A History* (Dublin, 1993)

Brown, Gordon; *Handbook of Fine Brandies* (London, 1990)

Cambrensis, Giraldus (Gerald of Wales); *The History and Topography of Ireland* (c1188; English translation, London, 1951)

Doyle, Lynn; *The Spirit of Ireland* (London, 1935)

Dublin Distillers; *Truths About Whisky* (London, 1879)

Irish Distillers Ltd; *The Story of Irish Whiskey* (Blarney, 1993)

Jackson, Michael; *The World Guide to Whisky* (London, 1987)

John Jameson & Son Ltd; *Soverigne Liquor* (Dublin, 1950)

Long, John; *A Treatise on Malting* (Dublin, 1800)

Magee, Malachy; *1000 Years of Irish Whiskey* (Dublin, 1980)

McCreary, Alf; *Spirit of the Age: The Story of Old Bushmills* (Bushmills, 1983)

McGuffin, John; *In Praise of Poteen* (Belfast, 1978)

McGuire, E.B; *Irish Whiskey. A History of Distilling in Ireland* (Dublin, 1973)

Morewood, Samuel; *A Philosophical and Statistical History of the Inventions and Customs of Ancient and Modern Nations in the Manufacture and Use of Inebriating Liquors; with the Present practice of Distillation in all its varieties; Together with an extensive Illustration of the Consumption and Effects of Opium, and other Stimulants used in the East, as Substitutes for Wine and Spirits* (Dublin, 1838)

Morrissey, James; *Hot Whiskey* (Tralee, 1989)

Morton, H.V; *In Search of Ireland* (London, 1930)

Murphy, Brian; *The World Book of Whisky* (Glasgow, 1978)

Nettleton, J.A; *The Manufacture of Whisky and Plain Spirit* (Aberdeen, 1913)

Philipson, John; *Whisky Smuggling on the Border* (Newcastle, 1991)

Ryan, John Clement; *Irish Whiskey* (Dublin, 1992)

Selected Papers and Manuscripts:

Bonner, Brian; *Distilling — Illicit and Otherwise — in Inishowen* (Donegal Annual 8, 1969 pp 74-97)

Cambrensis, Giraldus; *Expugnatio Hibernica* (c1188, Opera vol. v, ed. J.F Dimmock, Rolls, 1867)

Connell, K.H; *Illicit Distillation: an Irish peasant industry* (Historical Studies No3, 1961)

Ffrench, J.F.M; *On an Ancient Still-Worm discovered in the Co. Wicklow* (Royal Society of Antiquity of Ireland Vol 1, pp242-42, 1890)

Gaddesden, John of; *Rosa Anglica* (c14th century, Merton College, Oxford)

HMSO; *Abstract of the Scotch and Irish Distillery Act* (1823)

Holmes, John; *Monasterevan Distillery. A Brief Outline of its History and Background* (Kildare Archaeological Society Journal, Vol 14, pp480-87, 1969)

Kerr, J.J; *Aeneas Coffey and his Patent Still* (Dublin Historical Record, Vol 9-10, 1946-49, pp29-36)

Lumsden, Samuel; *Letters of Samuel Lumsden 1813-1818* (Public Record Office, Belfast, D.649 (1-14))

Ulster Journal of Archaeology; *On the Early Use of Aqua-Vitae In Ireland* (1858, Vol 6, pp283-295)

Ulster Journal of Archaeology; *On The Antiquity of Brewing and Distillation in Ireland* (1859, Vol 7, pp33-40)